Carolyn Lewis was born in Cardiff and has been living in Bristol since 1987. She is married with three daughters and one stepson and has seven grandchildren. Carolyn has been writing since she was eight years old. After leaving school, she trained as a journalist for the South Wales Echo and Western Mail, leaving to have her children.

Returning to work, she became a press officer for a number of organisations including Mencap. During this time, she began writing short stories, winning a number of prizes and awards. She co-founded a women only writing group which ran successfully for five years.

In 1993, following major spinal surgery, Carolyn embarked on a part-time English degree course at the University of the West of England, attaining a 2:1. In 1999, immediately following graduation, she applied and was accepted on an MPhil in Writing at the University of Glamorgan. Since her graduation, she has taught creative writing, taking workshops into local schools, adult education centres and has also worked for a drug rehabilitation project in Bath. Her novel *Missing Nancy* was written as part of the MPhil, and was published in 2008 by Accent Press. She is the author of *The Novel: A Perfect Recipe* (a guide to writing your first novel). She also writes short stories for *Woman's Weekly*.

D1354973

Published in paperback by SilverWood Books 2012
www.silverwoodbooks.co.uk
This book is a SilverWood Original – traditional publishing at its best

ISBN 978-1-906236-32-8

British Library Cataloguing in Publication Data
A CIP catalogue record for this book is available
from the British Library

Set in Trade Gothic by SilverWood Books

THE SHORT STORY

A guide to writing short stories

Carolyn Lewis

SilverWood originals

Contents

Introduction

Short stories are gaining a growing audience of readers and listeners. It has often been said that reading short stories is an economical way to discover unfamiliar writers: the time investment is minimal, the potential gains are enormous. There is a ready market out there for the budding short story writer to tap into.

Writing a short story can be demanding. You'll need the same ingredients as you would for writing a novel: characters, dialogue, a plot, a beginning, a middle and an end. The obvious difference between a short story and a novel is the number of words used. A novel can be anything between 70,000 and 150,000 (and may even be as long as 300,000!). A short story can be anything up to 7,000 words. And there's another difference: the need to make every word count. That's the challenge of writing a good short story, each word must bring something to the story. There is no room for superfluous words, each one must work for its keep.

Think about the following:

> *Short stories can offer the artistry and intensity of a poem; the themes and weight of a novel and all in a space so small that there is nowhere to hide a single error. No smoke and mirrors, no tricks. Character and narrative have to be developed as they would in a novel, but from a standing start. Sweeping, lyrical, brisk, photographic, still, psychological, miniature, savage – the short story's possibilities are close to endless.*

I didn't write that, it came from a recent article in *The Independent* which also said that short stories play a vital role in our literature. Their brevity and intensity might make them uniquely suited for the age we live in. I began writing short stories before I wrote novels and I truly believe they are an important part of our literary canon.

The *Encyclopaedia Britannica* defines the short story in the following way:

> *A brief fictional prose that is shorter than a novel and that typically deals with only a few characters. The short story is usually concerned with a single effect conveyed in only one or a few significant episodes or scenes. The form encourages economy of setting and concise narrative, character is disclosed in action and dramatic encounter but is seldom fully developed.*

The phrase 'concerned with a single effect' is particularly relevant, and something to keep in mind when writing your short stories. VS Prichett's description of a short story is 'something glimpsed from the corner of the eye, in passing'.

In the story entitled Community Life, Lorrie Moore has written, 'There was a blaze in his eye, a concentrated seeing. He seemed for a moment able to look right into her, know her in a way that was uncluttered by actually knowing her. He seemed to have no information or misinformation, only a kind of photography, factless but true'.

This is a superb example of that phrase, 'concerned with a single effect'.

I've come across a number of students who mistakenly believe that short story writing is easier than writing a novel. It is not.

The short story is a distilled literary form. Readers need to be captivated by the very first sentence. To hold a reader's attention, a story has to take them into a reality other than everyday life, and that reality has to be convincing. Narrative and character have to be developed as they would in a novel, but from a standing start. The short story form can offer the artistry of a poem, the themes of a novel, all engineered into a small space.

Writing short stories is complex, and I believe the short story to be one of the most challenging forms of literature. Having said that, this book has been designed to break down some of those challenges, to find out the best way to write a short story, to make every word count, to leave the reader with a sense of having read something remarkable. There is nowhere for the writer to hide in a short story, no room for sloppy writing or muddled thought. A short story needs to be able to tug on the reader's emotion and appeal to their senses.

In this book, I aim to demonstrate the best way to write a short story, how to develop them as an art form and how to learn the elements of the form. I will look at the best way to create believable characters, write life-like dialogue, develop the plot and keep to a reasonable word count. Everything must work to push your story forward: dialogue, characters and description.

Short story competitions regularly attract entries from all over the world and I will also discuss how to prepare your story for a competition, how to write within the designated word limit, and the best way to pitch your story to potential publishers.

Carolyn Lewis BA(Hons), MPhil in Writing

Before You Start

Before this book begins, I would like to offer two pieces of advice.

First, always carry a notebook with you. Listen out for the overheard phrase, the interaction between the people you see around you. Write down what you see, what you hear. It's been said that writers don't have holidays; we keep working, watching, listening the whole time, wherever we are. Look out for the bizarre and the curious, but don't forget the mundane. The ordinary also has its place in your writing.

My second piece of advice is to write something every day. This can be daunting; you sit at your desk or table staring at the blank page or empty screen and you don't know where to start. There are ways around this but it is important that you write every day. Build up a writing habit, tell yourself that you'll write for ten minutes, half an hour, or maybe you will write 100 words, then creep up to 500.

When my students tell me they don't know what to write about, I suggest, as a writing exercise, that they write, without stopping, about a room that holds significance for them. It might be where a grandmother lives, where a marriage proposal was made, a hospital ward, a classroom on the first day of school. I ask them to think about the room. What colour carpet does it have? Are there pictures on the walls, or is there a smell associated with the room? Then I suggest they begin writing.

What nearly always happens when embarking on this exercise is that a wave of memories will come flooding in. You can see the room, you can smell the room. Once that has kick-started the process, as the memories return to you keep on writing.

Having said I can give you two pieces of advice, there is a third I should like you to consider, and that is to keep everything you write. It might be that you don't want to show your work to anyone else. You may think that it's not polished enough, and that's fine. Only show your writing when you are satisfied with what you've written. The early attempts are important as they will help form you as a writer and it may be that, when you're writing regularly, you will be able to use your early work and incorporate it into a short story.

Part One: The Craft of the Short Story

1

Reading Short Stories

I would srongly recommend that you read a great many short stories. But if you're not familiar with the genre, where do you start? There are some wonderful stories by writers such as William Trevor, Raymond Carver, Alice Munro, Lorrie Moore, Helen Simpson and Annie Proulx.

These are writers whose work I really enjoy, but there are others equally as good: Chekhov, Elizabeth Bowen, Jane Gardam, Paul Gallico, Ernest Hemingway, Somerset Maugham, Guy de Maupassant, Tobias Wolf.

Read as many short stories as you can find. See how other authors go about their craft. See how they tackle the basics, the way they develop their characters, how they structure the plots, the setting, the denouement. And all of this within a reduced word count.

The best short story writers manage to convey their theme or message and you as reader will not be aware of the brevity of the narrative. You will simply enjoy the writing and feel involved with the characters.

Tania Hershman, editor of *The Short Review* and author of *The White Road and Other Stories,* says:

There is nothing more important for a writer of short stories than to read as many short stories as you can. Every time I find a new writer whose work I admire, I see what else it is possible for a short story to be, I am opened up to new structures, new ways of telling stories. I read hundreds of stories every year and am always amazed at how many of them I love, and how different they are from each other.

I can't better the following quotation from Raymond Carver in the forward to his short story collection, *Where I'm Calling From*:

This is what I wanted to do with my stories: line up the right words, the precise images as well as the exact and correct punctuation so that the reader got pulled in and involved in the story and wouldn't be able to turn away his eyes from the text unless the house caught fire.

When you read the short stories by good writers, see if that happens to you, that inability to turn your eyes away. If it does, that's what you too should be aiming for.

In 2009 Alice Munro was awarded the Man Booker International Prize for a body of work that has contributed to an achievement in fiction on the world stage. The following extract from her story *How I Met My Husband* will give an insight into her skill at short stories:

Sunday was a busy flying day in spite of it being preached against from two pulpits. We were all sitting out watching, Joey and Heather were over

*on the fence with the Bird kids. Their father had
said they could go, after their mother saying all week
they couldn't.*

*A car came down the road past the parked
cars and pulled up right in the drive. It was Loretta
Bird who got out, all importance, and on the driver's
side another woman got out, more sedately. She was
wearing sunglasses.*

The 'precise images' that Raymond Carver mentioned
are here: the woman who got out of the car 'all importance' is
exceptionally good.

I like the quotation from William Trevor who says that
whereas the novel tends to imitate life, 'the short story is bony
and cannot wander. It is essential art.'

2

What Sort of Writer Are You?

There are very many approaches to writing and it might be worthwhile to think about the sort of writer that you are:

- **The CAREFUL writer**
You've planned the whole story before you begin. You'll have worked out how the story will start, what happens to the characters as the story unfolds and you'll have already decided on an ending.
- **The writer with an IDEA**
This sort of writer might begin with an idea, something they want to share, a story with a message. If that's you, you'll build your story around the central theme you want to convey.
- **The writer who starts with a PLOT**
If this is you, you'll build your characters around the central plot, moulding them to suit the idea you have.
- **The writer who starts with the CHARACTERS**
You let your characters work with each other and then allow the plot to develop through the interactions between them.
- **The writer who IMPROVISES**
It may simply be that as you develop your writing, you find

yourself changing characters, changing the plot or altering scenes to improve characterisation. I am sure that there are a great number of short story writers who will say they come under this category. I think I probably come under this type too.

When I'm making a start on a new story, I try out different phrases, different settings, writing my thoughts in a notebook, testing the words I want to use. It's important to understand that there is no right or wrong method for writing a short story, it is simply finding out which one works for you.

Whichever writer you are, whatever type of writing suits you best, it is probably a good idea to assemble a plan, a sort of preliminary structure before you begin your short story. I would always recommend this for novice writers, as a way of focusing the mind.

The plan might be:
- What is my story about?
- What will happen to my characters?
- What is the pay-off?

Short stories are written to entertain, to engage the reader, so what is your story about? What do you want to write about? Is there an idea, a plot that you have been thinking about for a while? Maybe there's a situation that you have in mind, it could be that your story will be about something that happens to a fictional character, an idea that's been bubbling away for some time. If that's you, if you have an idea about what your story is about, write it down, give yourself an outline.

Next, what do you want to happen to your characters? Will they get what they want? Will something happen to stop them getting it? How will they cope with what you present them with?

And, finally, what is the pay-off? By pay-off I mean what is the message in the story, what did you want your story to say?

Generally short stories are about conflict, a discovery or a decision. There should be something of importance at stake for your main character. Don't be alarmed by the words 'conflict' and 'importance.' They don't have to mean something earth-shattering, they can mean something as ordinary as a job change. Think about the consequences that an over-heard conversation might have, a loaded glance between two people, revealing an intimacy, the finding of a document revealing a long-hidden secret or even something like the realisation that your character was not the favourite child.

3

Finding Inspiration

For a writer, inspiration is an interesting concept, something we need to develop, like antennae to pick up, to attract, to be ever alert for any idea, thought or something seen that we can make into a story. I believe that writers rarely take time off from being writers; we should always be alert, waiting to see, hear or read about something, anything, that we can use to write about.

Your inspiration might come from an idea you've had for a long time: something that happened to you or a family member. It might come from something you've read. At the time of writing this, it was reported in the national press that an Italian man had turned up at his own funeral. That would make a good short story, and one with plenty of scope. In particular, you might focus on his feelings upon finding out everyone thought he was dead. How would his family react to his appearance at the graveside? Another news item also caught my eye: a taxi driver searching for his passenger, an elderly woman who had left a carrier bag in his cab that contained £13,000. This is where your small notebook comes in handy: write down the things that interest you, something you've seen or overheard. Learn to ask yourself if something you've jotted down could be made into a short story.

Does it have enough impact? Can it be developed into an original and compelling narrative?

The irritating thing about inspiration is that sometimes it will arrive out of the blue, and other times, no matter how hard you try, it does not come. There is no magic wand to wave here, other than to suggest a break in your normal routine. You might find something inspiring if you see different places or meet new people.

I've found a number of ideas from listening to people talk on radio. One programme I heard invited people to phone in about their collecting hobbies, the more unusual the better. One man telephoned to say that he'd been collecting coat hangers and that he didn't like the wire ones. Once I'd heard that, the image of a room full of hangers wouldn't leave me. The story I wrote based on what I heard on the radio programme has since been published and won three prizes.

I called my story *The Collection* and my central character was Trevor.

PG Wodehouse said that his tales began in all sorts of different ways. He would start to write and in the process, whatever it was he'd started off with would get lost. 'On other occasions, stories would simply come out of nowhere.'

There were always people, mostly men, huddled around the bar of anonymous hotels or silently walking the corridors, key in one hand, briefcase or overnight bag in the other. Trevor kept a soft holdall in his car and he carried this with him as he wandered through corridors. It served two purposes he thought: he looked as if he belonged in the hotel and, of course, on a successful trip he could put the hangers in there. They had to be wooden, the coat hangers must be wooden; gold lettering was a bonus,

21

but he'd never take wire coat hangers.

After each trip Trevor put the hangers in the white wardrobe, going in there when he knew Cheryl was asleep. He often stayed in the room for some time, moving the hangers against each other so he could hear the thud.

I think it is fair to warn you that if you've lodged the intention of writing a short story firmly in your mind, you've perhaps become fixated with this, which could become counter-productive. You may have put an almost insurmountable obstacle in your path. Instead, try putting the idea of your short story to one side and concentrate instead on what goes on in your life. Observe everything, listen to the conversations around you, watch what people do and take note of your own reactions. Do you have certain thoughts, certain responses which crop up frequently? By familiarising yourself with this, more often than not something will click and you'll say to yourself, 'that was interesting' or 'I wonder what happened next'. This might be the start of a new short story.

■ EXERCISE

If you're still struggling, try asking yourself the following and see where it leads:

1) What would you like to happen to you?

2) Has your life turned out the way you thought it would?

3) What was the worst day you've ever had?

4) Does that day look different in retrospect?

5) Go back to your childhood, what can you remember about a holiday or a memorable school day?

6) Were you ever an inpatient in hospital? What were your experiences like?

4

Research

Research isn't always necessary in short story writing. Indeed, you may not need to do any research at all. It may be that your story concerns something that happened to you or a member of your family, or you may want to write about the job you've had for the last thirty years and your understanding of the subject can't be bettered. However, if your plot concerns something that happened a long time ago – say you've set your short story during the war years – or if it requires some sort of expert knowledge, then research may be needed to get the details correct.

The internet is a fabulous tool for writers and is generally your first port of call when digging around for information. There is plenty on offer in the way of blogs, news articles, archives and academic journals. Be smart about the information you review, however, and always check your sources. Sites like Wikipedia can be extremely informative, but be aware that anyone can add information or edit material, so truth and quality isn't always guaranteed.

The library is another place for research. Certainly it is more time consuming than the internet but you are almost guaranteed to find something useful amongst the vast number of books on the shelves.

Research can sound quite heady but it may simply mean that you can scour family albums. (I once came across a shadowy figure in an old photograph and discovered it was an elderly cousin of my paternal grandfather who had been sent to Borstal for stealing and who was never spoken about.) It might be that someone you know, a neighbour, a work colleague, has an interesting background. I've yet to come across anyone who has refused to help in research that I've been doing.

A good short-story writer has an instinct for sketching in just enough background to ground the specific story.
Lynn Abbey
– author

Research might be needed too for background information on your characters. You may have a character who has worked in banking for many years, or who has a passion for deep sea diving. With appropriate research, asking questions, seeking advice, you can build up a believable background for your characters.

Bear in mind too that when devising your plot, you may need to double check that what you have in mind, whatever situation you will be putting your characters in, is still credible. It is worth remembering that, whatever your age, things change rapidly, so what was accurate one year, may not be accurate the following year so you need to keep abreast with the changes in the environment where your character will live.

5

Establishing the Theme

Theme should not be confused with plot. It's an abstract or philosophical idea that encapsulates what your story is about. That might sound complicated but it isn't. Think of well-known stories, for instance *Snow White*. Think about what the story entails and you will soon recognise themes such as 'triumph over adversity' or 'love conquers all'. Theme is also a matter of individual understanding, meaning that someone else may read another message into the story.

What is important to remember is that without a theme, there can be no story.

In the William Trevor story, *The Ballroom of Romance*, the story is about Bridie, a single woman in her forties who cares for her elderly father as well as working on the farm that has been in the family for a great many years.

The highlight of Bridie's week is a Saturday dance, the ballroom of the title. Once there, she watches as other women, all single, vie for the attentions of the men present.

With sudden clarity, Bridie realises that the man she has been dancing with, the man who has shown an interest in her for a long time, has flaws.

When his mother died, he would sell his farm and
spend the money in the town. After that he would
think of getting married because he'd have nowhere
to go, because he'd want a fire to sit at and a woman
to cook food for him.

She also understands that there is no other outcome
for her once her father dies. 'She would marry him because it
would be lonesome being by herself in the farmhouse.'

Arguably there could be a number of themes here:
'better the devil you know', settling for second best, or maybe
turning a full circle. Certainly in Bridie's case, the longed for
romance is unattainable, as living the life she does, there is no
opportunity to meet anyone else so she settles for the life she
has always known.

The Ballroom of Romance is one of my favourite stories
by William Trevor, charting the grinding monotony of Bridie's
life. At the end when she realises that there is no escape for
her, the character of Bridie resonated with me. I desperately
wanted her to break away, to find a better life. Attaining that
resonance in short stories is something we should strive for.

In the Ballroom of Romance, she felt behind her
eyes the tears that it would have been improper to
release in the presence of her father. She wanted to
let them go, to feel them streaming on her cheeks, to
receive the sympathy of Dano Ryan and of everyone
else. She wanted them all to listen to her while she
told them of Patrick O'Grady who was now in
Wolverhampton and about the death of her mother
and her own life since.

You might find that you have a very clear understanding
of your theme, or it may be that as you write, you discover

another central message.

When you next read a short story, try and identify the theme, see if it is indicated by the plot. When writing your short story, in particular remember that you should be aiming for a cohesive theme that runs smoothly throughout.

The thing I love about short stories is that you can really take people up and down and all over the place very very quickly. *AM Homes*

In my story *What If*, my unnamed protagonist looks at a man she thinks she knows. She is in a restaurant with her husband, they are there for a celebration, when the man walks in. Throughout the story, my character carries on with an internal narrative, questioning whether the man she sees is the one she once knew. The whole time she conducts this silent conversation, she keeps referring to her husband, what a good man he is, a source of comfort and support. And yet, at the end of the story, as the other man seems to be asking her something, my protagonist rises from the table and asks her husband to excuse her.

> *Once more I look over to you. Your wife is sitting upright, her hands are in her lap. As you look at me, there is a suggestion of a smile on your face, your head is tilted to one side. What? What are you asking me?*
>
> *I lean across to my husband and I ask him to excuse me. I tell him I won't be long and his face creases into a smile. I rise from the table.*

And I ended the story there. My theme throughout I believe is forbidden fruit, or maybe it's the grass is greener.

■ EXERCISE

On the subject of theme, try writing a few sentences on the following well-known phrases:

Every dog has his day

What goes around comes around

Winning isn't important, it's how you play the game

You can't keep a good man down

6

Plotting

Plotting can be daunting to many first time writers and I always tell them the same thing: we don't have plots in our lives, we simply do the best we can with what life has thrown at us. I think the best way to approach it is to understand that plotting is merely another word for what happens to your characters.

Plotting can be broken down into six parts:

- **Exposition**: the characters are introduced, the point of view is established and some background information is given.
- **Opening incident**: a problem is introduced that will directly affect the main character. With the introduction of conflict, the plot begins.
- **Increasing action**: the conflict is built up.
- **Main Action:** new, more complicated incidents are woven in; build up to the climax.
- **Climax**: the conflict rises to greater intensity; changes the course of events or the way the reader understands the story. This might be either an event or an insight.
- **Resolution**: Ends the conflict, the reader is left satisfied.

The Cinderella story is a simple example of a plot that follows the six part rule.

- **Exposition**: In the opening scene, Cinderella is seen at the mercy of her step-sisters.
- **Opening Incident**: Occurs when the sisters receive an invitation to the ball and Cinderella's step-mother promises her she can go if she completes her chores in time.
- **Increasing Action**: The sisters taunt Cinderella and she despairs of ever going to the ball; but then her fairy godmother comes to her rescue and she's able to attend the ball.
- **Main Action**: Occurs when she loses her glass slipper.
- **Climax**: The Prince finds Cinderella and the glass slipper fits.
- **Resolution**: They marry, live happily ever after and the step-mother and sisters are punished.

Once you recognise these six points you will be able to see how other writers use them, to develop and play with plots. These points are only meant as a guide, something to steer you through the plotting, but I believe they are useful for a new writer.

It might also be useful to keep a plot outline nearby. You may already have one in mind and if this is the case, try writing down the plot as it unfolds.

Begin with the introduction of your main character:
- What will lead him to conflict?
- What initial conflict does he encounter?
- What action brings the conflict to its greater intensity?
- What is the climax?
- What happens as a result of the climax?
- What is the end result?

You will find that as you answer these questions you will have an outline of your short story.

A note of caution: remember that story events are best presented in chronological order, showing a cause-effect relationship. Another way of putting this is to allow one event to cause the next, which causes the next, and so on. When you are writing your plot outline, check to see that you have demonstrated this effect.

If you're struggling, unable to think of a plot, it's important to recognise that there are rarely any brand new plots. If you're writing a murder story, someone gets killed, someone else is punished, lives are changed. This as an idea has been done many times.

What you should always remember when writing is that although the plots have been done a million times before, what publishers are looking for is the new approach. A different angle to the tried and tested format of a murder story. Originality is the key word; bring something different to the story. If a character has been shot, tell the story from the person who sold the gun to the murderer. If you're writing about someone losing their job, write about the man who is making the redundancies. Tell the story from his viewpoint.

Whilst there is ample space in a novel to use sub-plots (extra dimensions to the main story), I would strongly recommend that you avoid them in a short story. Doing so runs the risk of overloading the story with too much information. Similarly, avoid including excess explanation and backstory, as every detail should have relevance to the plot.

I found the following quotation from Helen Simpson and I think it's relevant to this section on plotting:

The only rule I've ever been able to come up with for short stories is "something's got to happen, but not too much". A lot of it is knowing when to linger and elaborate — and when to keep quiet. It's best not to start with an explanation, a life history, or a big lead-up and filling in of background. That's the beauty of short stories, you don't have to include the usual boring stuff, you can just skip all that and cut to the chase.

■ EXERCISE

Try writing an outline for a plot. Keep a note on the six point plan and see whether your plot conforms to those points.

7

Characters

Fiction writers often find characters for their short stories from an amalgamation of people they have seen or known. They might of course simply be made up, a figment of the author's imagination, but usually characters are drawn from a mixture of real and imaginary people. Think about the people you work with, think about your neighbours, a distant relative, maybe the plumber who came to fix a dripping tap. There might be someone you see in the supermarket or in the queue at the Post Office. Any one of these could be the foundation for a character. If you blend what you have seen with a healthy dollop of fiction, you should have an interesting character to work with. That is one of the reasons why I write, that heady feeling as a character comes to life, the gradual build up, layer after layer, fact after fiction until I've got a well-rounded character.

As a short story writer, you face a challenge when creating your character. You have to conjure up a fully developed character without the benefit of a huge amount of description. The challenge is to search out the right detail – a speech pattern, a physical trait, a gesture – to convey a sense of who that person is, and in only a handful of words.

When writing short stories, it is a good idea to keep the number of characters to a minimum; three, perhaps four at the most. Remember that in short stories, believable, motivated characters can make or break a story. If readers cannot believe in them, or accept them, nothing else commendable about your short story matters.

When you have a character in mind, begin with a blank sheet of paper and head it with the character's name. Bear in mind that, like everything else, names go in and out of fashion. An 82-year-old man is unlikely to have a name like Darren or Justin. Equally a nine-year-old girl is more likely to have a name like Freya or Amelia, than Maud or Elsie. When searching for names, I often read through the Births, Marriages and Deaths column in the local paper. Some interesting and unusual names can be found there and the internet is another good place to search.

Once you have your name, make a start on writing what you know about your character: his age, his job, his appearance. Go further with this and write down his marital status, where he lives, what he eats for breakfast. What radio station does he listen to? What newspaper does he read? Go deeper into this character. Ask what sort of personality he has. How does he interact with the people around him? Is he an optimist or a pessimist? His education? His hobbies? What is his relationship with his parents? What does he sound like when he talks? What motivates him? What gets him out of bed in the morning?

In short, write down anything and everything you need to know about the character you've created.

It's more than likely you won't use all the information you've collected but it's important to remember that if you don't know your character well, maintaining consistent characterization will be almost impossible. You need to know his previous history, how and why he behaves in each situation. You need to know what he is capable of, whether he can adapt to these situations. You will have heard the phrase, 'a well-rounded character.' It is that roundedness that you must aim for.

To begin with, when describing your characters, it is worth sticking to the rule that the descriptions should only be included if they add something to the character. A simple example of this would be if your character is a man of high energy, who is never still. You might want to describe him as short and compact, who waves his hands around when talking. This way, physical description can add to the general personality of the character. However, the thing to remember when describing characters in a short story is that physical descriptions are not as important as personality traits.

Remember my earlier statement, that every word in a short story has to count. You don't have the leeway to waste words on superfluous description.

Think about how best to help readers see and know the characters. Indirect description can often be more effective than direct description.

An example of this might be:

She was scruffy.

How much better is:

The heel on her shoe was broken and her elbow poked through the hole in her sweater.

Think about using action to tell readers about your characters. Watching people's behaviour means we can learn about them.

Example:

He said he was pleased to see her.

A better way of putting this would be:

When he saw her, he smiled and enveloped her in a glorious bear-like hug.

Very often in a full-length novel, the character can be a cypher for you as author; in other words, an everyman. When writing a short story, the protagonist can really be anyone; they can be irritating, unsociable and maybe not the sort of person you want to share a 300-page novel with. In a short story they can be complete strangers and are all the more vivid because of it.

There are no bit parts in a short story, every character has to be there for a reason, to serve the story.
Tania Hershman

I'm often asked about the way to write disagreeable characters. All you need to concentrate on is making them believable; they don't have to be likeable.

The trick here is to try to get your readers empathising with the character. Even a thoroughly unpleasant character can have a reason for behaving the way they do. If your character is in prison, jailed for murder, write about the fact that he is unable to have access to the library where he feels comfortable. Without believable characters with realistic responses to their circumstances, you run the risk of losing your readers' attention and interest. It's important that, as a writer, you believe in what you write and in what you put your characters through. If you do your job well, your characters, your story, will take the readers into a reality other than everyday life.

To make a success of your story, you should be aiming to engage the reader, not just in your plot, but also with the protagonist. Readers want to experience what the character experiences and must sympathise and relate to the character as early as possible in the story.

I said earlier that three or perhaps four characters at a push are the maximum for a short story. Writing a sketch of each of your characters will help you to not only establish which is the central character, but also will help you to work out how they should interact with each other.

Just as you're familiar with the various personalities in your family or in your office, so you must know these people you've created. Learn their strengths and weaknesses, understand what makes them tick.

A word of caution: be careful to maintain consistent characterization all the way through, especially to the ending. Don't write a contrived change in your character to meet a surprised resolution to the conflict. I stressed earlier how important it is to aim for well-rounded characters. In the same way that you should know everything possible about your characters and the way that they might behave, you should also know the limitations imposed on them by the traits you've created for them. And, as people who we know well act in a manner we expect and predict, so your characters should also respond to the conflict of your short story in a way that follows on from what we've already learnt about them.

For instance, we would lose all empathy and trust in a character who we've come to admire and respect for their high moral values if they suddenly betrayed a friend without good reason.

Choosing the easy way to resolve the conflict in your story doesn't work as a quick solution; you'll let your characters, your writing and your readers down.

Now that you have a believable character, spend a moment checking that you haven't fallen into any stereotypical traps. Characters can be archetypes but not stereotypes. Archetypes are universally recognised prototypes or examples of a certain character type. They've been present in literature for centuries. By contrast, a stereotype is an over-simplification or generalisation of a type, and should be avoided in your central character. By conforming to stereotypes, your writing loses its edge and you run the risk of making your character weak or unmemorable.

Archetypes:
- The mother figure
- The star-crossed lovers
- The whore with a heart
- The flawed and brooding hero.

Stereotypes:
- The friendly vicar
- The genial landlord
- The homeless junkie
- The flamboyant homosexual.

■ EXERCISE

Try building up a word sketch of a character you have in mind. Use the suggestions I've put forward: list their hobbies, their fears, their understanding of the world. As with people you have just met, it will take time to get to know your characters, but that time will be well spent.

8

Voice and Viewpoint

Voice

As a writer, you must be able to create different voices, those of your characters. Voice in this context encapsulates the way the characters talk (dialogue) and the way they think (exposition). Each person will use language differently and even a fictional character has a voice that is unique to him. Though you're writing fiction you don't have to adopt a special literary way of using language. You can break the rules of grammar and 'good' English if you think it's necessary for the characters and the plot. You may have a character who drops the letter 'g' – talkin', nothin'. Maybe a character uses double negatives, 'I don't know nothing.' If this way of speaking forms part of the character, their background, their education, then it is perfectly acceptable to break the rules of grammar when they speak. I'd avoid too much rule breaking, enough and the character becomes life-like, credible, too much and the dialogue doesn't flow and detracts from the narrative.

Perhaps my phrase, 'breaking the rules' is too rigid, it might be better to think in terms of making allowances for dialogue, vernacular and less than perfect English.

A writer can use dialogue to particularly good effect by using the rhythms and lilt of regional speech. When planning your characters' voices you need to think about where they come from and how they sound. If you want your character to have an accent, think about the strength of it, and whether it could be easily portrayed. Be wary of using very strong dialects, as not only are they difficult to write, but it can often break up your dialogue, and be challenging for your reader to follow. The following extract is from Stephen Crane's *Maggie, Girl of the Streets*:

> *Let the damned kid alone for a minute, will yeh,*
> *Mary? Yer allus poundin' 'im. When I come nights*
> *I can't git no rest 'cause yer allus poundin' a kid.*
> *Let up, d'yeh hear? Don't be allus poundin' a kid.*

Crane uses strong vernacular spelling (phonetic spelling) in order to portray his Irish characters. He was writing in the late 1900s, when this style of writing dialogue was a lot more popular and often required. Nowadays we have much more of a melting pot of cultures, as well as access to media which makes finding examples of dialects much easier.

Remember, there is nothing worse than a dialect that sounds forced, false, or is out of touch, so it is worthwhile to do some research. Find examples of your dialect being used in everyday life; it could be a radio programme, TV show, or even a friend. Listen to how the accent flows, and note the phrases and colloquialisms that are used in speech. These are subtle aspects of language, and when used correctly, credit the reader's intelligence and ability to pick up on the nuances of the specified dialect.

As you explore you plan your story, consider making a character sketch and listen out for their distinct voices. Your character's speech pattern will be a part of their characterisation, not only in the dialogue but in the narrative of the story.

There are no rules with voice; it's more a matter of intuition. Ask yourself, 'does this voice sound right for my story?' As you develop a collection of voices, you will gain a greater depth and range as a short story writer.

Viewpoint

It's an interesting thought but with any given situation in real life, there will be more than one viewpoint, more than one perspective on what is happening. To use a cliché, 'there are two sides to every story,' often more. In terms of the short story, the point of view is the perspective from which the story is told.

So who is going to tell your story? Which character will you choose? This is an important choice for a writer to make because it's the viewpoint character that will win over readers and engages the reader in the story. You might have a strong central character that you want to tell the story. Alternately, the appropriate viewpoint for the story might not be evident at first. You may have to draft a couple of scenes from different characters' viewpoints until the correct one makes itself known.

The short story is traditionally written from either first-person or third-person, and the choice is yours.

First person viewpoint

First person viewpoint gives your writing a sense of immediacy, which can produce a greater impact than third person. First person is by far the most clear-cut, the 'I' telling the story from your protagonist's point of view.

> *I listened to Terry, I heard what he had to say, I heard the despair in his voice as he told me that his wife had left him.*

There are several ways to grab a reader's attention from the start – for example, a strong and distinctive voice, a bizarre and unusual opening, or throwing the reader straight into the action.
Tania Hershman

If you're writing a monologue in the style of Alan Bennett's *Talking Heads*, it will obviously be in the first person. Written this way, monologues have great impact and drama, giving the reader insight into the sole character's thoughts. Because they are so dramatic, monologues work very well on radio and there is a section on writing for radio at the end of the book.

The reader can only experience events through this narrator's eyes. Information and other events in the story will have to be reported back to the protagonist, so if your plot is a complicated one, there may be a great many ploys for letting the reader know what the other characters are doing. Such ploys might include phone calls, visits, reflections on conversations with other characters.

Third person viewpoint

In first person you have an insight into and an understanding of the central character. In third person you have access to the thoughts and emotions of all the other characters. If you choose to work in third person, you will use 'he,' 'she', and 'they'.

It could be argued that third person lacks the immediacy and familiarity of the first person, but writing in third person does offer a writer tremendous scope. Your characters can go wherever they like and you can place them wherever you choose.

I wouldn't recommend writing a short story with multiple viewpoints. Rather than writing about three or four characters, choose a central one and write from his viewpoint. It is easier to write from one perspective and you will find the word limit on your story more achievable. Multiple perspectives and stories have the potential to create complications and higher word counts. This is not to say that you should avoid them altogether, but I would advise gaining a confidence and strength to your writing before experimenting further. Once you've written one story, you might feel confident enough to tackle a different viewpoint – maybe a story with four characters, all of which have a story to tell. Having said that, I would always recommend to students that they stick to a single point of view when writing a short story.

'Limited omniscience' is when you write in the third person, but are limited to one character's world, their experiences, thoughts etc. In Alice Munro's story, *Walking on Water*, the central character is known only by his surname, Mr Lougheed, and the story is written entirely from his viewpoint.

> *A little while after the incident in the downstairs hall, Mr Lougheed had come home one day and found a sign painted on his door. It was something like a flower, with thin red petals, inexpertly painted, and black petals in between, tapering the wrong way.*

By writing from this perspective readers stand a better chance of identifying and empathising with one central character.

Whichever viewpoint you choose, be consistent throughout the story. Don't chop and change perspectives. Otherwise, there could be nobody to 'tell' the story, it could be muddled and the reader may become confused.

A brief mention of second person and third person omniscient.

In second person viewpoint, the prose speaks to 'you' as in this example:

> *You walk down the hall, you can hear the clock ticking, the hum of the refrigerator, you don't know if there is anyone else in the house.*

I would strongly recommend avoiding the use of second person in a short story, certainly for a first time writer. Writing in the second person is unusual and can be demanding. There are very few examples of short stories written in the second person, which is probably as good a testimony as any for not using it.

However, Jay McInery, Carlos Fuentes, Nathanial Hawthorn and Michael Butor have written stories using the second person, read their work, see if you agree with me.

The third person omniscient viewpoint is not complicated. It simply means there is another all-seeing, all-powerful voice telling the story. However, third person omniscient can have the effect of confusing the author's voice with the narrators. I've had a number of students who fall into this trap. For example:

> *Mrs Jones sat by the fire, she pulled the blanket towards her face. Winters are hard for old people.*

In this case, the author's voice is in the sentence, 'Winters are hard for old people.' That's the author's view, not the character's.

To avoid the pitfall, try putting the thought as coming from the character, Mrs Jones.

> *Mrs Jones sat by the fire, she pulled the blanket towards her face. She knew people didn't understand how hard winters were for old people.*

As a technique, third person omniscient was used by writers such as Jane Austen and can be found in many 19th century novels. However, it is best avoided in modern short stories.

■ EXERCISE

Try writing in first person; compose a two-page dialogue. Get inside the character's head and project the immediacy of the 'I' who is telling the story.

Now re-write the same pages, this time from the third person.

See which viewpoint you prefer, which gives you greater scope.

9

Dialogue

You have your characters, now you need to let them talk. Dialogue is merely another word for conversation and for a lot of writers, it's a challenge and one that must be tackled if you want your characters to sound realistic.

I would say too that writing convincing dialogue is arguably the hardest skill a writer needs to develop. Short stories depend on dialogue not only to promote the reader's understanding of the character, but also to rouse their imagination. For all of us, whether fictional characters or real life people, the way they speak opens up their personality and we can learn a lot from someone's conversation.

Dialogue is a useful tool for a writer as it can be used to convey the plot and to keep up the pace of the short story. Every word that characters say in a short story has to achieve three things: advance the story, produce some change in the other person and allow the speakers hidden self to show through.

Over the page, there is a passage from Jane Gardam's story, *The Latter Days of Mr. Jones*, in which a single man causes concern as he watches children in the park. Not a word is wasted in conveying a depth of meaning within the dialogue.

I'm afraid there are a lot of allegations, sir. One woman seems to have jogged the memories of others. We've been working on this case for a long time. The neighbours are not happy. Some of them have children.

In the conversation, a lot of information has been revealed; information designed to propel the story forward through the use of dialogue.

You can also use dialogue for dramatising an incident, by showing the reader the trepidation your character is feeling.

I can't tell you why, I just know you have to leave.

Be aware of the words not spoken, the hidden meaning, the sub-text. This can be done by describing body language. If your character is acting defensively, show how he sits with his arms crossed over his chest, or maybe how he avoids eye contact. Techniques such as these, combined with dialogue, will enable your reader to see an instant picture. They will understand the hidden message, the tensions that are implicit in the dialogue between characters.

Remember that each time a character begins new speech, you should begin a fresh line. Do not lump each of your characters' voices in the same paragraph. To add yet another reason for getting to know your characters properly, it should be obvious from the way each one speaks exactly who is talking. There should be a definite difference between them. An example of this is from an Alice Munro story, in the anthology *The View from Castle Rock*:

'You know that time I got caught coming out from under the apple tree?' I said, to my own surprise.

'Yeah.'

'I told her I was looking for a bracelet, but it wasn't true. I went in there for another reason.'

'Is that right?'

By now I wished I had not started this.

'I wanted to get under the big tree when it was all in bloom and look up at it from underneath.'

He laughed, 'That's funny,' he said. 'I wanted to do that too. I never did, but I thought about it.'

You will see from this example that there is a clear difference between the characters. We know who spoke, even though we do not know the characters' names. By using a new line each time a character speaks, there can be no confusion about who's talking.

When writing dialogue use exclamation marks sparingly. Over-use will mean your characters sound as if they live their lives in a state of hysteria. Even more importantly, when you do need to use one, your previous usage will have weakened its meaning.

Take time to think about the way your characters might speak.

- Do they have verbal tics?
- Is there a favourite phrase they use?
- Can you tell if they're well educated or not?

This careful attention to detail is another reason why it is so important to know your characters thoroughly. You need to demonstrate how he will speak in a way that is absolutely consistent. If your character is a teenage girl, would she have an inflection in her voice, one that causes her voice to rise at the end of each sentence, as if she was asking a question? If your character is an older woman, maybe she speaks with hesitancy, searching for the right word. You're the only one who can do this, who can give your characters believable dialogue that matches the type of people they are.

When we speak, our conversations are often rambling, repetitive, relying heavily on a lot of 'you know' or 'like', and if you write dialogue in the same way, with no sense of it ever coming to a conclusion, your readers will be bored to tears. What you must strive for is believable, purposeful conversation between your characters, words that flow without superfluous chat.

Another point to remember is that dialogue not only conveys meaning, drives the plot and carries information, it also gives readers evidence of the reaction to remarks made by other characters.

For example, if your character tells his wife he wants a divorce, you might want to write that in response, 'her jaw dropped'. By using this technique you are adding to the dialogue, demonstrating the effect their words have on those around them. If your characters are having a full-blown argument, their words ricocheting around the room, write about the way they use their hands, the angry, furious gestures they'd make, for instance:

> *Her finger jabbing at his chest, she yelled, 'You! You're useless.'*

It is worth noting here that when writing about an argument, people tend to use short sentences which carry far more dramatic weight, the words darting from your their mouths like bullets:

> *'No, get out!'*
> *'I'm going, you make me sick.*
> *'So go, leave me alone.'*

It's fairly obvious that these characters are having an argument and in these instances, there is no need to pile on more dialogue; here as in so many areas of writing, less is more.

You can also add descriptions that will help readers to hear the tone of voice:

> *He lowered his voice, 'Take your time.'*
> *He adopted a formal tone, 'We need to think this through.'*

A word here on attributions, also known as dialogue tags.

These are the words writers use to follow speech; for example, 'he said' and 'she said', and can help distinguish who is speaking.

A writer at the beginning of their career will try and avoid repetition at all costs. This can lead to substituting staple 'said' tags for words like 'whispered', 'shouted', 'and 'yelled', or even 'expostulated'. You might feel that by using less familiar words, you are proving that you have a wide vocabulary. In fact, all it does is point out that you are a new writer. An experienced writer knows that the simpler words are by far the best when it comes to dialogue tags.

Commoner terms such as 'said' contribute so little meaning when reading text that the eye basically skims over them and they become almost invisible, allowing the reader to concentrate on and become more deeply involved with the dialogue. However, the less common the term, the more it will stand out and distract the reader from the content of your story.

This is not to say that you should never use 'other' dialogue tags, but I would advise using them sparingly, and description here and there can help to emphasise a character's speech, for example:

> *'Get away from there!' he bellowed.*

Avoid using attributions like 'she laughed' or 'he smiled', for example:

'You are so ridiculous!' he smiled.

Needless to say it is practically impossible to 'smile' words, let alone 'cough' or 'chuckle' them. If you can't physically do it yourself, don't give it to your characters to deal with.

Punctuation also serves as descriptive tool when writing dialogue, and is more effective than using embellished tags:

'Wait!' Anna exclaimed.
'What?' James asked.

The exclamation mark and the question mark tell the reader how to interpret the speech, and the words in the tags become superfluous. If you feel more description in required, look at how the actions of the characters can influence the dialogue.

'Wait!' Anna said, clutching desperately to James' coat as he stepped onto the train.

The most important point is that a good writer will employ devices such as scene setting, context and description to enhance dialogue, and create an image for the reader. By doing so they avoid having to fall back on superfluous words and clumsy phrases that detract from the quality of their writing.

When writing dialogue
Test it to see if it has texture and depth by reading it aloud. Listen out for the word that needs emphasising or the phrase that should be spoken softly.

Check for inconsistencies in the names, or whether there are superfluous words. Does the dialogue sound right for your character?

Are the words you've used appropriate for his age, his background, his job? Is the conversation stilted or does it ramble?

A stylistic note here on dialogue: when writing a word that carries emphasis, put that word in italics so the reader knows that this is a strong word:

> *When I tell you to do something, you will do it now.*

The most important thing to take from this chapter is just how essential it is to achieve a clear difference between your characters, which is predominantly demonstrated through dialogue. As previously mentioned, you can only do this well if you've done enough work on your characters. You've written about characters who are so individual that there can never be any doubt about which one is speaking. Aim for that; the recognisable speech pattern of each character without you having to state who is speaking. You should have written your lines of dialogue so convincingly, your readers know which one of the characters is speaking without you spelling it out.

EXERCISE

With the characters you've already created, write about an argument between them. Try to use dialogue not only to add drama but also to propel the plot forward. See if you are able to write so well that it is immediately obvious which one of your characters is talking without you naming them each time.

10

Descriptive Writing

Good descriptive writing should be a vital component of your short story, enabling your readers to vividly imagine the story unfolding before them as they read. When using description, remember that readers will want to experience what you have written by relying on their five senses: sight, sound, touch, smell and taste. All of these can be achieved by understanding how to use descriptive writing for the best effect. When you are writing about what is seen, heard, and so on, remember to emphasise the details of what is being experienced to give the narrative as much atmosphere and realism as possible.

Read the following two examples:

Walking through the long grass, Julia felt hot. She needed a drink, something cold.

and then compare it to the following:

Julia had been walking for two hours, the dry over-long grass tickled at her bare legs, the sun burnt her forehead. She groaned, she needed a drink,

something cold with ice cubes clattering against the
sides of the glass.

The first example is brisk and spare, with no detail to give the reader any idea of what Julia is thinking and feeling.

But in the second example, through the use of detail, we get a much stronger sense of Julia's discomfort. We can feel the heat of the sun on our forehead. We hear the sound she makes as she longs for a cold drink, we can smell the over-long grass as it bakes in the sun. We can imagine how the grass feels tickling her legs. We can even taste the cold drink, almost feel the ice cubes against our teeth.

When choosing and using descriptive words a good writer will use specific nouns rather than general ones. An example of this is:

The woman pushed the heavy trolley out of the
busy supermarket.

And then:

The elderly woman urged the heavy trolley away
from the crowds mingling at the door.

Also:

He walked out of the room.

And then:

He strode towards the door; he wanted to leave the
room.

With your descriptive writing you should be aiming for

a technique called 'Show don't Tell'. You must show the reader, not merely tell them what is happening. Bear in mind that readers will rely on a visually arresting image, so you should do your best to display the story to them through description. Simply telling your reader the action will never create an image as clear or immediate as showing them the manner in which events take place in your story. By choosing words such as 'strode' or 'urged', a much clearer picture than 'walked' or 'pushed' is created. Choose your descriptive words carefully, and remember that you have a limited word count in a short story so each word must matter and bring something to the plot.

'Show don't Tell' should be used for all aspects of your writing. If your character is in a dirty room, show how dirty the room is. Describe the sink full of unwashed dishes, the stains on the floor, the smell of the overflowing waste bin.

Avoid using bland words such as 'pretty,' 'handsome', or 'untidy.' An image is what you're aiming for, something that your readers can see and that will nudge their imagination.

Helen Simpson wrote of one of her characters that he had 'something of Belgium about him, the lack of life in the streets, the uncurtained windows'. That has stayed with me for a long time.

'Show don't Tell' essentials:

- Create a visual image with descriptive language.
- Add dialogue so the reader can experience a scene as if they were there.
- Use sensory language, convey what your characters can see, hear, feel, smell and taste.
- Add action to bring your writing to life.
- Use action and movement to engage and involve your reader in an unfolding scene.

I think what is useful to remember is that description

can be used to heighten and strengthen the theme of the story. If your story is about an agoraphobic woman, use descriptive language to make the world outside her front door frightening, a large expanse of space she does not want to enter.

I also think that this is a good place to say that you should not be afraid of language. Use words that don't immediately come to mind, play with words, see what effect you come up with; not merely in description but also seek out words to heighten your story, to add depth, and to give the reader an instant image. Don't use flat words, choose different vocabulary. Stretch your mind, sound the words out, see if they fit in with your story. They may well add another dimension to your writing. Don't be afraid of using bold words or using language in an interesting way.

Cliché

A cliché is a remark or an idea that has been overused to the extent that it has become unoriginal, meaningless and stereotypical. Whether writing a novel or short stories, clichéd words and phrases should always be avoided. Do eyes always sparkle? Will a laugh always be tinkling? Should something be avoided 'like the plague' and is skin always like a 'peach'? It is essential to search out new words, fresh descriptions, a fully realised word picture that will stay in your reader's mind long after the story is finished.

Obviously, not all descriptive words are clichés. Your job as writer is to search out the best ones you can find, to offer a new slant on an established theme.

There are not only clichéd words, clichés can also be found in plots:

- Secretary having an affair with her boss.
- A single parent who splashes her last £5 note on a scratch card – and wins.

- The finding of true love through a lonely hearts column.
- The acquisition of a puppy or kitten to heal a broken marriage.
- A thief who has a sudden burst of conscience and returns the stolen money.

As with so many aspects of writing, originality is what you should be aiming for, something new, a different slant. It's important to steer away from the obvious.

Metaphors and similes
Metaphors and similes are an excellent way of enhancing your descriptive writing by expressing the resemblance of one thing to another. You'll find them in most forms of creative writing because they contribute to the imagery, playing on the reader's imagination as they read to bring vivid, realistic pictures into their minds eye.

A simile is a figure of speech in which one thing is compared to another, using the word 'like' or 'as.'

This is from Helen Simpson's story, *Millennium Blues*:

People had mouthed at her like earnest goldfish.

The following is from Lorrie Moore's story, *You're Ugly Too*:

The monitor was in place and Zoe's insides came on the screen in all their grey and ribbony hollowness. They were marbled in the finest gradations of black and white, like stone in an old church or a picture of the moon.

A metaphor differs from a simile as it compares the same things by saying something actually is that object instead of using 'like' or 'as.'

In a metaphor from Lorrie Moore's story, *Dance in America*, a house is described as being 'one of those beautiful wind-tattered billboards one sees in the Californian desert.'

I've used the following metaphor in the short story I'm currently working on:

> *Nicholas stared at his wife, where was the woman he married? Where had she gone? In her place was this large, shambling person: unruly hair and a body the shape of a fridge.*

Metaphors and similes are useful tools for a writer to master and offer another way for bringing images to your reader's mind. The trick is to keep things simple. An over-complicated comparison will draw the reader's attention away from the story. It is immediate recognition you're aiming for, something that readers will identify with.

As with all aspects of writing, the concept of 'less is more' is especially true when using descriptive words, metaphors and similes. It is important when writing a short story that you are able to bring an image to mind using as few words as possible.

Qualifiers

Qualifiers are words that slightly alter the meaning of others, words such as 'often,' 'very' and 'almost'. These words rarely add anything to the narrative and, in fact, can weaken your story.

When you read through your work (and we'll be discussing how to edit further on in the book), cut out these unnecessary words, unless by doing so you run the risk of fundamentally changing the meaning of the sentence.

On the subject of getting rid of unnecessary words, it seems like a good place to mention getting rid of superfluous adjectives. I've come across several that deserve a mention:

- Tearful crying
- Gentle embrace
- An affirming nod.

Crying is tearful, an embrace is gentle and a nod is affirming. There is no need to say it twice.

In a short story you have no room for unnecessary words so weed them out, guard against them at all times.

■ EXERCISE

Describe the inside of a bakery, focusing on the smell and the sight of the fresh bread. Use descriptive words to bring the interior of the shop to life.

11

Using Flashback

A flashback is a quick, economic, and effective way to show important character history and events, without delving into the whole back-story. The most common use of flashbacks is to demonstrate something that your character has done before their appearance on the page, something that might explain their behaviour in the story.

Flashbacks are an easy tool to use. You simply write as if you were writing a normal scene – the difference is that the action happened before the main events of your story.

A warning note about the use of tenses: when you go back in time, use the past participle 'had' to indicate to the reader that they are entering a flashback. But only use the past participle twice when you introduce the flashback, and then carry on in the simple past tense for the remainder of the flashback. An example of this might be:

> *Joseph remembered the first time he shoplifted. He'd been scared, his heart had thumped uncomfortably. His mouth was dry when he put the Cadbury bar in his pocket, but he dared not look back; his*

new friends waited for him outside, and he knew
they'd tease him mercilessly if he didn't produce
the goods.

You will see from this example that a flashback can convey information about something that happened earlier, and had some impact on the character's life, and can also be used to make use of your character's thoughts. Maybe it's something about their childhood that had an effect on them, in which case it is a simple matter to inform your readers of their earlier life.

Likewise as you enter a flashback using the past participle, remember to exit the flashback with two similar uses of the word 'had'.

It's easy to leave a flashback, to enter the present tense once again. This extract is from Raymond Carver's story *Cathedral*:

> *She'd worked with this blind man all summer. She'd*
> *read stuff to him, case studies, reports, that sort of*
> *thing. She'd helped him organize his little office in*
> *the county social-service department. They'd become*
> *good friends, my wife and the blind man. How do*
> *I know these things? She told me. His being blind*
> *bothered me, my idea of blindness came from the*
> *movies. In the movies the blind moved slowly and*
> *never laughed.*

Now, after telling you how best to use flashback in a story, I would also say keep a careful watch on how often you use them. Too much 'history' can kill the pace of your story.

It's a matter of keeping careful control of your word count, remembering that 'in a short story, every word must count'.

■ EXERCISE

Using a flashback, write a paragraph about a character that has lost his job. Describe the interview he undertook to get the job, and what his feelings were when he heard his interview had been successful. Link it up with his thoughts and feelings when he is dismissed.

12

Beginnings

Beginnings are hugely important in any piece of fiction. In a short story, the beginning takes on a significant weight as it must immediately grab the reader's attention. Also bear in mind that in a short story you do not have time for setting the scene over a number of pages, or giving your reader your central character's life story.

I believe there are certain points to be aware of when writing the beginning:

- It must catch the reader's attention straight away.
- It must draw the reader in.
- It must set up a conflict of some kind.

Read short stories, see how many times the story begins with dialogue or a dramatic event.

I've found beginnings from three short story writers and I've used them here as examples of the points outlined.

This is from Raymond Carver's *What Do You Do in San Francisco?*:

This has nothing to do with me. It's about a

young couple with three children who moved into a house on my route the first of last summer. I got to thinking about them again when I picked up last Sunday's newspaper and found a picture of a young man who'd been arrested down in San Francisco for killing his wife and her boyfriend with a baseball bat. It wasn't the same man, of course, though there was a likeness because of the beard. But the situation was close enough to get me thinking.

There is enough going on in this paragraph to lure the reader in, to keep them reading. It catches their attention whilst hinting at conflict.

Another example is from Lorrie Moore's story *Paper Losses*:

Although Kit and Rafe had met in the peace movement, marching, organising, making no-nuke signs, now they wanted to kill each other. They had become also, a little pro-nuke. Married for two decades of precious, precious life, Kit and Rafe seemed currently to be partners only in anger and dislike, their old, lusty love mutated to rage. It was both their shame and demise that hate (like love) could not live on air.

This is an extremely good example, establishing the earlier relationship and the current situation between the two characters.

The final example is from Helen Simpson's short story *Burns and the Bankers*:

They were sitting down at last. There were over a thousand of them. All that breath and flesh meant the air beneath the chandeliers had very soon climbed to blood heat despite the dark sparkle of frost outside on Park Lane. An immense prosperous hum filled the hotel ballroom, as if all the worker bees of the British Isles were met to celebrate industriousness.

I would defy anyone not to want to read more when faced with any one of these examples.

When beginning your short story, think about the ways you can entice a reader. It might be that you can use dialogue to reveal character and setting and, in doing so, it may lead to conflict. This example by William Trevor, from his story *Miss Smith*, captures the reader's imagination with use of dialogue and setting:

One day Miss Smith asked James what a baby horse was called and James couldn't remember. He blinked and shook his head. He knew, he explained, but he just couldn't remember. Miss Smith said, 'Well, well, James Machen doesn't know what a baby horse is called.'

She said it loudly so that everyone in the classroom heard. James became very confused. He blinked and said, 'Pony, Miss Smith.'

'Pony! James Machen says a baby horse is a pony! Hands up everyone who knows what a baby horse is.'

All the right arms in the room, except James's and Miss Smith's, shot upwards, Miss Smith smiled at James. 'Everyone knows,' she said. 'Everyone knows what a baby horse is called except James.'

James thought, I'll run away. I'll join the tinkers and live in a tent.

Here, the opening dialogue sets the scene so that we can feel James's discomfort. In this way we can ally ourselves with James, championing him.

You may want to begin your story by establishing the setting, by giving enough detail to create a certain atmosphere. We saw this in the Helen Simpson story and another example of this is to be found in William Trevor's story *Raymond Bamber and Mrs. Fitch*:

> *For fifteen years, ever since he was twenty-seven, Raymond Bamber had attended the Tamberleys' autumn cocktail party. It was a function to which the Tamberleys inclined to invite their acquaintances rather than their friends, so that every year the faces changed a bit: no-one except Raymond had been going along to the house in Eaton Square for as long as fifteen years.*

In this example, William Trevor has developed the setting as well as giving enough detail to create a particular atmosphere. An 'autumn' cocktail party implies a seasonal event that occurs throughout the year, and the fact that cocktails are considered an expensive 'frivolity' suggests that the Tamberelys are quite well off. They obviously have the money to put on such an occasion, so we are led to believe that they are high society. By inviting their 'acquaintances rather than their friends', the Tamberleys are cast in a vain light. These changing faces imply that there is a concern for appearance, and a desire to 'show off' to the wider social circle. However, the character of Raymond draws us further in to the story, as he has been attending the Tamberelys' parties, 'for as long as fifteen years.' His presence at these events is unusual but has become a long-standing tradition, and we are led to believe that there is something special about Raymond, that sets him apart from the Tamberelys' crowd. By using a few choice words William Trevor has managed to give the history of his characters, and leave his readers wanting more. This is an example of an ideal beginning.

■ EXERCISE

Re-read the previous extracts and note down how the authors have informed, and then engaged you. Using these devices try writing two or three beginnings for a short story. Remember, it is all about the economy of words so try and contain it to one paragraph.

13

Endings

As with the beginning, the ending of your short story should do the following:

- Realise your plot.
- Establish the change in your central character as a result of the conflict you've arranged for them.
- Create a satisfying ending.

There are many ways to end the story, and by far the most commonly used, is simply to resolve any conflict so the reader is content with the way things turn out. It is also a natural conclusion to the story telling convention of 'beginning', 'middle', 'end'.

In her collection *Ice-Cream*, Helen Dunmore's story, *Lilac*, tells the story of Christie, a 13-year-old girl sent to live with her aunt and cousins whilst her mother recuperates from a breakdown. The beginning of the story tells how Christie spends her time at her aunt's house, the lilac is in bloom and she sees, 'The new leaves flash and rustle. Everything was coming alive and it was the fastest, greenest Spring I had ever seen.'

The middle of the story concerns Christie's relationship

with her cousin, Tommy. Christie loved Tommy, 'Of course I did, it was natural. We were the same kind of person.'

Then one day, Tommy tells Christie that his friend Henrik is coming for the weekend and Christie sees them together, 'I saw Tommy, his head back, his eyes closed and Henrik kissing his throat'. She sees them under the lilacs and the following day she goes back to the lilac bushes. 'I pulled down a branch and buried my face in the cones of the flower.' Dunmore ends this story with the one line, 'I said nothing.' There is a natural flow to this story, a clear cut beginning, middle and an end.

You may wish to consider a surprise ending, something unpredictable. In his story, *The Necklace*, O Henry wrote about a woman who works most of her life to pay for a replacement jeweled necklace she borrowed and lost. Later, haggard from hard work, she once more meets the woman from whom she borrowed the necklace.

'You say you bought a diamond necklace to replace the other one?'

'Yes, you didn't notice? They really were exactly alike.'

Madame Forestier, profoundly moved, took Mathilde's hands in her own. 'Oh, my poor Mathilde, mine was fake. It was worth 500 francs at the most.' After reading this story, I felt a profound sense of pity for Mathilde, all that wasted effort.

If that is your preferred ending bear in mind that, whilst it may be unpredictable, it should still be consistent with your characterisation. Again, by getting to know your characters well, you can introduce a bizarre situation, or erratic behaviour, without it seeming implausible. To give an example of this, in his short story *Fireman*, from the anthology *Caravan Thieves*, Gerard Woodwards's characters behave in a peculiar manner:

> *So she placed the chamber pot carefully on the floor*
> *beside the table, stood up, pulled down her knickers*
> *and squatted over the thing. Erica peed into the*

chamber pot, filling it to the brim, as guests all
around the restaurant applauded.

Although the behaviour is bizarre, and although there is a shocking surprise, it is still believable because of what we've learnt about the characters and the way they behave.

I prefer an ending where the reader gets a sense of the characters' lives continuing once the story has finished. A master of this technique is author Raymond Carver. The following extract is from *Elephant* from his anthology *Where I'm Calling From*:

> *'Go' I said, 'What are you waiting for, George?'*
> *And that's when we really flew. Wind howled*
> *outside the windows. He had it floored, and we*
> *were going flat out. We streaked down that road in*
> *his big un-paid for car.*

Elephant charts the life of a man whose family continually takes money from him. The ending suggests his freedom from those demands, and there is a sense of his life becoming easier. The reference to the 'un-paid for car' could easily be interpreted as the character breaking the economic ties that have tethered him for most of his life.

It seems like an obvious statement to say that your ending should make sense: whether you opt for a 'happy ever after' ending, a twist in the tale or even leaving an open ending, it must be logical to the reader.

An ending should be one or two paragraphs long and it should bring the whole story together. It should answer any questions raised in the core of the story.

This might be the place to discuss 'twist in the tale' endings as these are liked by readers of magazines and short story judges. A key part of writing twist in the tale short stories is not to reveal the crucial line or clues too early. The later on in the story, the better it will be. Give clues but do not be too obvious. If readers can guess the outcome too soon, it is not going to be an enjoyable experience for them. The outcome has to be believable, if it is too weird, too strange the reader may feel cheated upon finishing the story.

Do not add a brand new character at the end as a way of solving or ending your story. It may seem like a quick solution but if you are going to use this type of scenario, go back to your story. Add something about this character at an earlier point in the tale, leave some false clues or hits. A story in a recent edition of *Woman's Weekly* tells of a lump discovered by a character, 'For the last ten months her life hadn't been her own.' The twist in the tale in this story was that it had been her husband who'd been diagnosed with cancer, not the wife.

Most importantly, remember that if you're aiming for a twist in the tale, avoid the clichés, steer clear of it was all a dream, it was really his twin brother. Remember to be different, originality is the name of the game.

In her acceptance speech for the Man Booker International Prize, Alice Munro said that she is not interested in happy endings but in 'meaning, resonance, some strange beauty on the shimmer of the sea'. As writers, that is what we should be aiming for that.

Ali Smith said of the ending of a short story, it 'isn't an end at all, but always a kind of beginning: the point where the story, having closed, opens for and in a reader like a germinating seed cracks open in the ground. An end, when it comes, should always send you back to the beginning, because a good story, like any real art, demands revisitation.'

With that quote in mind, I can offer a final piece of advice on endings: don't prolong it – say what you have to say and leave the story.

■ EXERCISE

Think about endings to stories you have liked, re-read them and note what makes them work and why you like them. Is there an ending to a story that you didn't like, or one that surprised you? Again note down your reasons and look at what devices the author has implemented to provoke this response. Now, try writing two different endings for the same story. How does this change the way your story is perceived?

14

Structure

In the section on plotting, I gave you a six-part format and in this section on structure, I want to focus on another format, an outline on how to structure your short story.

The rules of narrative that we learned in school literature classes apply to writers too. It's quite possible that you won't have room to hit every element of traditional plot structure but bear in mind that a short story is roughly composed of exposition, conflict, rising action, climax and denouement. By all means experiment, but remember that something has to happen in the story – at least the reader has to feel that something has happened. Dramatic devices such as conflict and resolution achieve this.

The art of story-telling may appear magical, but the building blocks are concrete. In essence, your story must have a beginning, a middle and an end.

If, when writing a short story, you try haphazardly to fix a number of bits together (random sentences, the odd piece of description), your story will not flow. There will be no cohesion and you'll leave the reader with a disjointed mess. If you've done your character research properly, there should be a rightness about what is happening to your character. Your story should evolve and grow out of its own internal logic.

This is another reason why you should read as many short stories as you can, to see how other writers structure their work; the way they seamlessly move from one sentence to another, a natural following on from what has been written.

Your story won't work if you write in odd sections explaining what is going on or filling in with additional pieces of background information.

A short story needs tension, the reader has to want to read on to find out something, so don't give everything away at the beginning...
Tania Hershman

A new writer often lacks confidence and I've come across many students who have doubts about what they want to say. Often new writers will add unnecessary bits of exposition in case the reader has missed the point. Confidence will grow but only by writing more.

I started this book by saying you should build up a writing habit; write something every day and your confidence will grow as a result of this. You as the writer have to appear confident in what you have written. If you don't, your reader will invariably sense it and lose interest in your story.

I am a great believer in reading work aloud. This way, you can hear where the story is weak, where the sentence structure is disjointed and bitty. Aim for a smooth flowing narrative, a natural progression from one incident to another.

Previously, I've suggested writing out your plot and charting the progress of your short story before you even begin writing. This might be a useful tool for you when checking out the structure of your story. I think it would be fair to say now that there are no set rules about writing, whether novels or short stories; it's more to do with finding the arrangement that works best for you.

Try this as a basic story structure:

A widowed, elderly man lives on his own, his days are dominated by the rituals he imposes: breakfast at 7.30 am. Lunch at 12.30 and his evening meal at 6.00 pm. Then, into his strictly adhered to routines, his estranged son makes an appearance. By the introduction of his son, the character of the father comes into the conflict that will challenge him in the story. Rising action might be that the son stays with his father, he has lost his home, his job and his apparent disregard for how his life is turning out, enrages his father. Climax could be a number of things: the son steals from his father or refuses to get out of bed before 11 am. There can be a number of ways to introduce climax into this scenario. Denouement might be a reconciliation between father and son, it might be simply that the son leaves and the father returns to his rigidly structured days.

This is just one example of a story structure that follows a variation on the six point rule. You might prefer to structure your story this way rather than adopt the strategy laid out in the chapter on plotting. So long as you build on a solid storytelling foundation (one that employs the three keys to any great story: hook, development, climax), you may vary the structure in whichever way suits the story, your characters and the plot. Simply find a solution that suits you.

■ EXERCISE

Try writing 8 – 10 sentences which tell the story of Ben, a 31-year-old who is having a crisis of some sort. He works in a factory and still lives at home with his widowed mother and her menagerie of cats and dogs. He desperately wants to move out but knows that his mother relies on him. Go into his thoughts, his moods, work out what conflict there would be for him.

15

Setting

Setting is an all-important ingredient for creating a good story. It is the world that surrounds your characters, and the environment they interact with. You could even think of it as a character itself, in terms of research and development, and presence within the story. Remember that a good story doesn't necessarily require grand or exotic locations as a backdrop. As a writer you are creating an atmosphere, and whether your characters are on a Miami beach or sat in an empty room, setting a good scene will really help your story come to life.

Setting can include the weather, the furniture in the room... but be wary of excessive description, which can make a setting seem 'static'. Static settings lack life and verve; they run the risk of losing the reader. On the other hand, an 'active' setting can engage the reader, with vibrant and lively description.

Compare the following two paragraphs:

Example A
The small black bird with the brilliant red wings and inquisitive yellow eyes perched on the white picket fence just out of reach

of the tabby coloured cat with a scar on his leg and his one eye half-closed, scarred from some long ago fight.

Example B
The red-winged blackbird glided in for a landing just as the battle-tested tabby cat leaped up, claws out, to intercept it. Catching the edge of one of the bird's wings a single loose feather floated down to the garden path. A few feet away the bird landed safely on the fence.

Example A is static, **Example B** is active. It is easy to understand why A is flat, static and why B is active, engaging the reader. There is vibrancy and suspense, followed by a sense of relief that the bird escaped.

There are three questions to ask when you're considering the setting for your short story:
- Is setting important to the plot?
- Is setting important to the characters?
- Is setting important to the theme?

In an exercise I set my students, I ask them to write about a couple as they travel from Lands' End to John O'Groats in a vintage Chevrolet. In this case, the setting is the car and I ask my students to write about the significance of the Chevrolet. Does the fact that it's a vintage car put pressure on the characters? What brought them to the car? How do they feel about their journey? Why are they making it? Indeed, as mentioned in the first paragraph, the car itself could be thought of as a character. The car is old, it will need to be driven carefully, nurtured on its journey, and this sets up a range of actions for the characters.

Within the confines of a short story word count, you may not have the space to create exotic locations with long descriptions of blazing sun, crashing waves, or endless vistas of snow-covered mountains. Try instead to let the characters interact with the setting so that the reader can see it through the eyes of the narrator, as in this example from Jane Gardam's short story *The Fledgling*:

> *She drove cautiously through a treeless desolation of pink tarmac, tentatively round weedy roundabouts. Mud and workmen's tools were everywhere. Cement kerbstones held back rubble and were ticketed with signs and arrows for the future. In the distance, there seemed to be a complex of drab, prefabricated single-story buildings. This was the wider world that Stella had been so proud that Lester was clever enough to inhabit.*

This is a superb description of the view a mother has of the university where her son will attend. The 'treeless desolation' she sees mirrors the desolation she feels as she drives him there, taking him away from home. The imagery of a construction site can be seen as a metaphor for Lester (the fledgling), constructing a life for himself through education.

Whether your story is set in Terminal Four of Heathrow Airport, it's important to give your setting vibrancy, a fresh perspective that makes your readers look again at the commonplace and well-known.

■ EXERCISE

Try writing a paragraph about a couple who have been running a small shop for thirty years. Write about the stifling confines, the feeling of suffocation, and the boredom that either the husband or wife feels. Make the shop the symbol of their despair.

16

Style

Style is often referred to as the author's voice. This should not be confused with the character's or narrator's voice or with writing in first or third person. The author's voice is simply the writer's style, the way you write.

Style is an amalgamation of a number of things including syntax, dialogue, figures of speech and imagery, punctuation and word choice. It is how you arrange these things that will determine your particular style.

Writing is a highly personal occupation – we bring so much of ourselves to our prose and it is this 'personality' that we should strive for when we write.

When I urge students to read as much as they can, I listen as they tell me they are concerned they might subconsciously copy the author's style. There is a huge difference between being influenced by an author's style and directly copying it. We all absorb what we read. We look at the way the characters are portrayed, the way the dialogue has been handled, and we probably do subconsciously take parts of someone else's style. However, it's highly unlikely that you would copy another author's style and, if it did happen, your writing would be jerky and unnatural. I have given students exercises where I've asked them to write like Raymond Carver or Alice Munro and the outcome is always the same: students tell me their writing felt awkward and constrained.

In each of my classes I set homework for students and, before long, I can recognise each student's style. Without looking at the name on the sheet of paper, I know immediately which homework comes from which student. They invariably start off the lessons timidly, unsure of whether they're capable of writing but it isn't long before their confidence grows and they develop their own highly individual style.

You may have to write a lot before you realise that you've found your style; it might be that you need to make a number of starts before you understand what your writing style is. It will be unique to you and as individual as the way you speak.

I hope finding your own style comes easily, but if you feel unhappy with the way you've started on your story, I would suggest trying it again, loosening up the dialogue and altering the narrative. See if you're more comfortable with that. I suggested at the beginning of this book that you aim to write every day, because the more you write the sooner your confidence in your writing will evolve and so too will your style.

Over the years students have asked me time and again about their writing style: "How will I recognise it?". My answer is always the same: "Trust me, you'll know when you've found it!"

17

Time Span

The Passing of Time

The short story is just that, short. My advice is to limit the time span in your story to a short period of time, a week, two days, maybe even an hour. There is little scope within the constrictions of a word count to allow your story to unfold over a period of years. There are very many extremely good short stories where the time span covers the events of one day in the central character's life.

In his story, *Collectors*, Raymond Carver writes about a man who has a visitor, a salesman who arrives at his house and shampoos the carpet. The story takes place over the period of time that the salesman is there: an hour, maybe two.

> *I found the ashtray. He took it, dumped the contents onto the carpet, ground the ashes and cigarettes under his slipper. He got down on his knees again and inserted a new filter. He took off his jacket and threw it onto the sofa. He was sweating under the arms. Fat hung over his belt. He twisted off the scoop and attached another device to the hose. He*

adjusted his dial. He kicked on the machine and
began to move back and forth, back and forth, over
the worn carpet.

Carver has packed a lot of detail into this extract. We know that the salesman is determined to demonstrate the cleaner, he's assembled it competently; by the use of the word 'kick' we know he's anxious to get the demonstration started, and we know he's overweight and sweating.

The Passing of Time:
There are ways to depict the passing of time, devices to show the reader that time has elapsed since the story began.
　　To return to *Collectors*, Carver writes:

Once in a while I looked out of the window at the
rain. It had begun to get dark.

The reader is made aware that whilst the salesman is working on the carpet, time is moving on.
　　It's a simple technique, you might want to write about the ticking of a clock, the arrival of the 11.30 train, or use the technique William Trevor uses in his story, *An Afternoon.*

Across the road, a delivery van drew up. No one
got out and a minute or so later, it drove off. A dog
went by. A woman started a lawnmower in one of
the front gardens.

In this story, one character waits for another and whilst waiting, these mundane events are observed. The words are simple but they convey that time has passed.

Although the time span can be short, this does not mean that little happens in the short story. Drama and epiphanies are there, as are moments of clarity. These epiphanies, or 'moments of revelation' are useful in short story format as they sum up a culmination of events in a very short space of time.

Try to use the events you depict to illustrate your theme. By this I mean, use the epiphanies in your story to reflect your general theme. You might be writing about someone finding their long-lost brother, the meeting that eventually takes place, the realization that, after years of searching, the newly-found brother is not, after all, a likeable person. The epiphany here would possibly be that it was the thought of discovering someone who'd been lost, someone who might have contributed to the family and yet the family was pretty much complete. This might reflect on the theme of appreciating what you already have.

I've mentioned the William Trevor story, *The Ballroom of Romance,* before and on the subject of time spans and epiphany, I will return to it as an example. The story takes place over a few hours and the epiphany is there, right at the end of the story:

> *She rode through the night as on Saturday nights*
> *for years she had ridden and never would ride again*
> *because she'd reached a certain age.*

The character's epiphany is both the climax and resolution. This story had a considerable effect upon me – the realization that whilst Bridie had been chasing dreams of finding someone to marry, someone to take her away from her stultifying existence, these dreams would never be realized and, whilst mourning the loss of her dreams, I had the sense of her life continuing the way it always had been. Maybe it was enough for her to have had the dream. Read it for yourself, see if you agree with me.

18

Word Count

If you're writing a short story for a specific market, a magazine or a competition – maybe it's one story in a proposed collection – first of all check the small print.

If the magazine stipulates a word count of 2,000 words, then that's what they want. Not 2,500, not even 2,100. The maximum is 2000 so make sure your story isn't a word over. Many competitions will state very clearly that they are seeking entries with a specific word count and you must respect that. A lot of stories, many of them well-written, will be rejected because the writer didn't adhere to the word count.

> **The only thing a short story is required to be is short. Apart from that, anything goes.**
> *Tania Hershman*

Trade magazines such as *Mslexia* and *Woman's Weekly* will always give their preferred word count, and it is up to you to write within that limit. In my experience, the majority of magazines and short story competitions seek short stories of 2,500 words, and it can be a challenge to write within that number. Don't think that as you're only one hundred words over it won't matter. It will matter; you must get rid of those extra words. Surely it's better to give yourself a chance of being published or winning a competition by sticking to the word count?

■ EXERCISE

There are a number of short story competitions with a word count of 100. This is a real challenge: to form your character and tell your story within such a limited word count.

Try it yourself; see if you can get your story to include a beginning, middle and an end all within 100 words.

19

Micro/Flash Fiction

Micro-fiction or flash fiction came into popular usage in 1991 although it can be traced back to proverbs and the shortened narratives of Aesop's fables. Ernest Hemingway's best known micro-fiction is 'For sale: baby shoes, never worn.' The brevity of this prose adds to the power of these six words. And that's the secret behind micro-fiction, the telling of a story in a much reduced word count.

As a general rule, flash fiction is between 300 – 1000 words. Longer than micro-fiction which is 10 – 300 words, significantly reduced from traditional short stories. It might be worth thinking about the fact that flash fiction is usually a story of a single act, sometimes the culminations of several unwritten events.

At the beginning of this book, I said that, in a short story, every word must work for its keep and in micro-fiction, this takes on far greater interpretation. Try to remember that, with a word count as low as 100, you don't have any room for wastage. You cannot take two pages to explain all that happened before the story began. See if you can put it in the first paragraph – then write the rest of your story.

On a similar vein, start in the middle of the action. A woman is running, a bomb is about to go off. Don't describe any more than you have to. Readers can fill in some of the blanks.

Concentrate on one powerful image. It might be a car crash, a swollen river. As with all writing but particularly so with micro-fiction, you're aiming to paint a picture with words.

A good tip for writers of micro-fiction is to use references to a commonly known story. By doing this, you save yourself a lot of unnecessary words. Use famous situations, an obvious example would be the sinking of the Titanic. The minute your reader sees the word Titanic, without your explanation, they know what is going on. If you feel Titanic is too obvious, use other well-known situations, the driving test, the buying of a house, start of a new job. All those will have been experienced by most readers, so their knowledge saves you the trouble of painting a picture for them, their own understanding will fill in the blanks.

There is usually a twist ending to micro-fiction, allowing the writer to pack some punch at the end of the story. There is good reason for this, with the brevity of word count, there isn't enough time to build up sympathetic characters or to show how a long, complicated plot has affected them.

A writer new to me is Lydia Davis and she was recently interviewed by the *Times* and she said, when asked about her very short stories, 'I'd say that a sentence alludes to a narrative. Many readers have told me that the short ones really grow in their minds and what is missing is supplied.'

In her collection of stories *Break it Down*, the following story is entitled, *The Mother*.

> *The girl wrote a story, 'But how much better it would be if you wrote a novel,' said her mother. The girl built a dollhouse. 'But how much better if it were a real house,' her mother said. The girl made*

a small pillow for her father, 'But wouldn't a quilt be more practical,' said her mother. The girl dug a small hole in the garden. 'But how much better if you dug a large hole,' said her mother. The girl dug a large hole and went to sleep in it. 'But how much better if you slept forever,' said her mother.

A perfect example of the blanks I mentioned earlier, the relationship between mother and daughter, the ending, loaded with inference and drama. There is a gradual build up here, leading to the mother's last statement.

With the advent of texting, many people have acquired the art of using few words to get their message across and the *Times* held its own Twitter micro-fiction competition last year. The winning entry was:

Tenderly he slipped the ring on her finger. 'Grow old with me, my love.' She agreed, not knowing he meant right away.

A number of writers have published anthologies of micro-fiction, amongst these are Dave Eggars' *Short, Short Stories* and Dan Rhodes' *Don't Tell Me the Truth About Love.* If this style of writing appeals to you, then I would strongly recommend you read examples of the style, see how other writers cope with a much shortened word count.

EXERCISE

Write a story in 100 words with loss as its theme.

20

Titles and Themed Stories

Titles

Have you chosen a title for your story? Sometimes a title won't arrive until you've finished the story and sometimes you've had an idea before even beginning writing. If no title occurs to you, don't agonise over it. It will come. There will be a phrase or something one of the characters has said that will inspire you. However, it might be that a title still evades you when you've written, edited and polished your story.

If that happens, try playing with the words. Maybe it simply means you use a character's name as the title: William Trevor's stories *Mr. McNamara* and *Mr. Tennyson* and Jane Gardam's story *The Latter Days of Mr. Jones* are all such examples.

Or maybe the theme of your story can produce a title for you. I recently had a story published in *Woman's Weekly* that I titled *Some Sort of Twilight* because I thought it represented the muted world the central character was living in.

If all else fails, try using a working title until the right one pops into your head. Don't work too hard or get anxious over it; something will occur to you – and when it does, you'll know that it's exactly right. This is what your story was meant to be called!

Themed Stories

When I mention themes again, this is not a repeat of the earlier chapter when I discussed the theme of your story; this is something entirely different. If you're writing for a short story competition, sometimes the organisers will suggest a theme. A recent North Somerset organisation called for stories on the theme 'Shadows'. A competition I entered last year had 'Silver' as its theme. When I'm working with my students on stories for competitions, we normally brainstorm ideas, working out as many suggestions as we can. Like every other aspect of writing, you need to be original and find a different take on the word.

In my class we thought about shadows: what did they mean to us and what angle could we adopt to incorporate them into a story? We came up with the following:

'Living under the shadow of an older sibling'.
'Under the shadow of redundancy'.
'A family living under the shadow of a terminal illness'.

I was aware when we were discussing them that the word 'shadow' had dark connotations and certainly the subjects under discussion were not positive, and so we then talked about ways to make them more positive. One student came up with a good theme, that of a young man who in the early 60s went to a concert to see Cliff Richard and the Shadows, an event he kept quiet about as most of his friends were Beatles fans.

When you have been given a theme, search out the unusual and steer away from the original way of looking at the subject. Do adhere to the theme. Don't send in work that does not comply or else your story will be discounted.

More than once, a student will say that they're writing a

collection of stories on a particular theme – it might be marriage or loss of a family member. Each one of Helen Simpson's stories are on a theme: in her latest collection *Getting a Life*, her stories are centred on the 'blisses and irritations of domestic life'.

The trick here is to have something original to say in each one of the stories. Although there might be a central theme, each story needs to stand on its own merit.

■ EXERCISE

Work on a 500 word piece of writing with communication as your theme. See what you can come up. What original slant can you find?

21

Editing

Once you've finished your story, you may feel that you should leave it for a while before editing it. I agree that putting some distance between you and your story can be hugely beneficial. But don't leave it for too long – a day, maybe a week. Any longer and it can be difficult to get back into the process. When you do come back to it, take your time reading, go over it slowly, but still don't edit it just yet. Simply read, see if the story engages you. Be prepared to feel disappointed – this happens to most writers. What you had wanted to write might not bear any resemblance to the story in front of you.

On the second reading, arm yourself with a pen or marker and work through the story, making notes and checking to see if the characters are believable. Does the dialogue ring true? Is the theme apparent? Put a line through the areas that need work.

Ask yourself the following questions:
- Will the beginning catch readers' attention?
- Do the actions of my characters fit their personalities?
- Is the setting suitable for the characters?

- Did I select the most appropriate point of view?
- Is it consistent?
- Does the conflict result from likely causes?
- Have I shown and not told?
- Does my sentence structure add emphasis and variety?
- Is the ending rewarding?
- Have I resolved the characters' conflicts?
- Have I used too many words?
- Have I made each word count?
- Have I got a 'precise image'?

These are only a few questions to ask yourself, but there's one that's probably the most difficult to answer and yet it's one of the most important. Is this a satisfying read?

When editing you need to be ruthless. If a phrase or word adds nothing to the narrative, eliminate it. Could you use a more vivid verb than the one you're currently using? Or maybe very plain verbs work best for this story. By reading your story a few times, you will get a feel for it. Does it have a rhythm or is something missing?

If the story begins too slowly, you may be starting the story too far back. In this case you might consider cutting unnecessary background information.

When editing you need to be ruthless. If a phrase or word adds nothing to the narrative, eliminate it.

- Is the dialogue overlong? Remember the 'less is more' mantra.
- Have you repeated things? Does it need to be said twice?
- Look at the way your plot moves. Is there enough to keep the reader turning the page? Can the pace be improved upon? Is there too much description and not enough action? Does enough happen?
- How are your characters shaping up? Have you

described the colour of their eyes, rather than the kind of person they are?

When writing a short story for a specific market, a competition or an anthology with a limited word count, you need to cut back until your story not only makes perfect sense but it does so in its leanest form.

Look at the following sentences:

Martin felt an uncomfortable lurching in his stomach, his mouth was like cotton and he felt sweat break out under his arms.
(22 words)

Now after editing:

Martin's stomach lurched, his mouth was dry, his underarms were damp.
(11 words)

The meaning has not altered but by getting rid of superfluous words and rearranging the order, the number of words in the second sentence is halved.

Try to maintain a sense of perspective when editing; true, there may be aspects of the story that don't work, but equally there will be some that work very well. A tip I often bear in mind is to begin my editing with the strongest part of my story, the part I like the best, and work outwards from that. It might be that you work better when you concentrate on the weakest parts. Other times you might have to begin your editing at the end of the story and work on making it as dynamic as the beginning. Don't be afraid to try different beginnings and endings before you arrive at the best one.

I think it's fair to say that editing takes far longer than actually writing the story. You might have to re-write it four or five times before it's perfect.

Check grammar and punctuation. Many writers think that it will be someone else's job, an editor or publisher or competition organiser, to correct their grammar and punctuation. Don't make this mistake. As a new writer, your aim should be to present your work in the best possible format. There are many writers who mistakenly believe that the power of their writing will overcome sloppy grammar and bad spelling. If you're writing for a competition, your story needs to be well presented and without any mistakes. If you don't take care of mistakes, your work may well be discarded.

Check the tenses in your story – have you used them properly? Are they consistent? Look at the way you've used commas – are there too many? A wrongly placed comma can change the meaning of a sentence, so be careful. A common mistake I often see is when an author fails to put a comma before the name of the person they're addressing.

What would you do, David?

Also check that you've kept the name of your character consistent throughout the story. In a story I wrote for a competition, it was only after the third reading that I realised I'd changed the character's name halfway through.

Check that you've correctly used apostrophes. Have you put in too many exclamation marks? Have you used italics properly? Identify clichés and weed them out. If you're unsure about the grammar, maybe now is the time to let a trusted friend read the story. Often a second pair of eyes will spot things that the writer has overlooked. There can be no excuse for misspelled words. Have a dictionary on hand if this is something you struggle with, and by all means use the computer spelling and grammar checker on your computer. But don't rely on it 100 percent. In short, be diligent. Be aware. You've worked hard to complete your story, so don't let yourself and the story down with sloppy editing.

During your edit, you can also run a check for any alliteration that occurs. By alliteration I mean the repeated use of one letter. 'Peter picked up the paper'. In this case, the letter 'P'. Once this is read out loud, the alliteration is obvious and can sound comic where no humour is intended. This is the sort of writing that appeals to very young children so if that's your target audience, fine. If not, amend it.

A student of mine had written an excellent short story but there were examples of alliteration, 'When Susan saw the sea, she smiled'. With a few adjustments, a brief discussion on what the student wanted, we changed the sentence to read: 'When she saw the waves moving towards the beach, Susan laughed.'

By the time you feel you've done enough on editing, you probably have. To go over it one more time is not only tiring, it's counter-productive. You need to have a sense of when the time has come to leave it alone.

Part Two: Problems and Other Issues

22

How Stories Can Go Wrong

Stories can go wrong in many ways... the characters lose their way, the plot meanders off course, there's no planning or structure, the prose becomes overblown, the grammar, spelling and punctuation let the writer down. Be honest with yourself and look at your story with a critical eye.

Some common problems:

Lack of Engagement
One of the main reasons some short stories fail is because of the writer's inability to engage the reader. The success of a short story or any piece of fiction relies heavily on the reader fully engaging with the character. The reader needs to experience what the protagonist experiences, and that engagement must begin as early as possible and carry on as the story develops.

We all read to experience someone else's life. Therefore chart the progress, or lack thereof, as your characters develop and we follow their lives. It is this rapport, this connection that you should aim for when you write your characters' stories.

William Trevor in his short story *Flights of Fancy* describes a character this way:

> *At forty-seven Sarah Machaen was reconciled to the fact that her plainness wasn't going to go away. As a child she'd believed that growing up would put paid to the face she couldn't care for, that it would develop prettily in girlhood, as the ugly duckling had developed. 'Oh, it's quite common,' she heard a woman say to her mother, 'Many a beauty was as plain as a pikestaff to begin with.' But no beauty dawned in Sarah's face.*

This section appears in the second paragraph of the story and immediately there is a connection; we sympathise with Sarah and need to know what happens to her. As a technique, this works extremely well: as readers we're instantly drawn to Sarah thus ensuring that we will turn the pages in our desire to follow her progress.

Overwrought prose

Good short stories should be a series of events: conflict, action, resolution, the last occurring when the character(s) experiences either a change in thought or an epiphany moment. To achieve this you have to employ good word choice, fresh images and a coherent thought progression. A good short story cannot be achieved if you slide into abstract ideas and over-blown prose. If you've written your story using flowery language, there is a strong possibility that your prose will become more important than the story.

This is not to discourage the writer from using clear, beautiful language. There will be occasions in your story when lyrical prose can be used as characterization or to illuminate a point. The danger lies in over-egging the story, bringing in complicated, inflated prose in the mistaken belief that your reader will understand and appreciate your command of language and fall in love with your cleverness rather than the story and characters.

Again, go back to reading short stories by some wonderful writers. Observe how they use words and how they bring images to life with simple, dramatic phrases. A mantra for all writers is 'less is more'. It's worth remembering that far more impact can be made by the use of simple, everyday language that readers can understand and appreciate.

Overblown and complicated language runs the risk of eroding the story and making it unreadable. Clever prose is, of course, subjective, but be aware that when clever prose becomes an irritant, the majority of readers will stop reading or lose interest in what you've written.

While good detail is an essential element in any story, keep in mind the 'less is more' mantra particularly in your use of adverbs and descriptive words. Too many can deaden the impact of the prose, and so offset the desired effect of a story. Therefore, rein in the temptation to over-emphasise description.

Consider this description of a table:

The table was badly scratched. There was a deep indentation down the middle, the edges had marks where cutlery had scraped, and stains caused by red wine and innumerable cups of tea decorated the top. One leg was shorter than the others.

This example is not so much a description of a table as it is a list, which is boring to read. Far better to say:

The table was scratched, one leg was shorter than the others and the top bore the marks of family life.

Your reader will fill in the rest; they will instantly know

what you mean by 'the marks of family life'. As writers we must give our readers room to imagine the world we've created, enabling them to see the characters and the setting we've put them in.

There is an extremely good example of the 'less is more' technique in Jane Gardam's story *Blue Poppies*:

> *Clare House stands blotchy and moulding and its doves look very white against its peeling portico. Grass in the cobbles.*

With a few well-chosen words, the scene has been set. There is a clear image of the dilapidated Clare House. As I said earlier in the book, make every word count, make it earn its keep. Try to keep things direct and simple.

Irrelevance

When developing a story there are unlimited choices for character motivations and actions, which the author must make. Every single one of these decisions supports and drives the story. As an author, you need to be in control of the creation of your story. Ideas bubble up from a lifetime of experiences, and their significance is revealed late in the writing as an afterthought.

Be aware that relevance only comes from thorough planning of what will happen in your story, how characters react to conflict and how that changes their way of thinking. Aim for reader enlightenment, which, when different from the character's enlightenment, could be the source of important ironies.

For most of us, when we read, we read something in the story that is related to an emotional experience we've had. Emotion and its intensities vary from story to story and might include fear, joy, sympathy and anger. Emotions are best evoked when the reader is completely engaged, rather than when the reader feels merely like a listener, an extra.

To achieve this, you must show emotion in the narrative. Rather than simply describe the events of the story and the characters' blunt thoughts, infuse the narrative with subtle description of how the characters react to events. Show don't tell, but in that showing, the reader should be able to discern what emotions the characters are feeling.

When AL Kennedy's latest collection of short stories *What Becomes* was published in 2009, one reviewer said:

> *One paragraph (in the collection) might also be a manifesto for the genre in general: a short story can be a track that speaks to you personally, that you read over and over again. Finding out what happens in a short story is over so fast that it scarcely matters. What matters is that you hold the prose in your head, re-read and reconsider it. A short story has to be well made to withstand that kind of attention. With so few words, not one can be wasted. That is why they are difficult to write.*

Your aim as a writer should be to master the craft of dramatic prose, the result being that the reader remembers the characters long after the story has finished. This too links in with Alice Munro's comments about wanting to achieve resonance at the end of each story.

In her story *Family Man*, Annie Proulx writes of an elderly man living in a care home in Wyoming. He has kept a long-hidden family secret and believes the time is right to tell his granddaughter of the secret. When he does, she fails to understand the significance and the last paragraph records his disappointment in her.

> *'That's the one I loved,' he said, knowing it was hopeless, that she was not smart and she didn't*

understand any of what he'd said, that the book he
thought he was dictating would be regarded as an
old man's senile rubbish. Unbidden, as wind shear
hurls a plane down, the memory of the old betrayal
broke the prison of his rage and he damned them
all, pushed the tape recorder away and told Beth she
had better go back home to her husband.'

The story revolves around Ray, the elderly man, his life and the secret he has kept hidden all his life. The secret has shaped his life, the decisions he's made. The disappointment he feels when his only surviving family member fails to understand what he's told her is a triumph from a well-respected short story writer.

Timing

The trick with timing is to learn how to balance the events in your story. Have you got all the action in the first 400 words? Does the rest of the story limp along to the end? Careful timing is vital. When you reach the climax of your story, there should have been a gradual build-up, a layering to reach this point. Be ruthless when you read through your story – does it flow, does one event move smoothly on from another?

If you've taken on board the section on structure, you should be well on your way to having a perfectly timed story: exposition, conflict, rising action, climax and denouement. If you feel that your story has been rushed, go back to the beginning, re-write the introduction, pace the disclosures, allow for gradual enlightenment. That's not to say that the opening should be drawn out and laborious, not at all. Aim for realistic disclosures, a natural progresssion of events.

I think this is a good place too to say that as with all aspects of fiction writing, be prepared to re-write, to pare down, to change. You're on a learning curve and you can only learn by adopting a flexible attitude to your writing. If something isn't working, learn to recognize that you can improve it, you can change it. Nothing is cast in stone, if you think you can write it again and make a better job of it, then do it.

Filling up the story

I've known students who have jammed far too many topics into a short story. They have something to say and they feel that whilst they are at it, they can include a lot more. I believe a short story carries far more impact if it has one central theme. Check that you've not meandered off the path and included a diatribe on global warming or battery farming which maybe has huge importance to you but has no relevance to your central plot. Remember the mantra, less is more.

Time span

We discussed this at the beginning of the book and check to see that you're not covering too large a time span. In her story *Queenie*, Alice Munro covers a period of 30 years but this is a writer of huge talent and experience and she gets away with it. My recommendation would always be for a restricted time span for a novice writer; time to experiment when you've written as much as Alice Munro!

Too many characters

My advice at the beginning of this book was to limit the number of characters in your short story to three – four at the most. It might be that you've ignored that and have added more characters, believing that their stories needed to be told. A short story simply cannot carry the weight of too many characters. It will become top heavy, over-loaded with dialogue and different points of view. Characters will be clamouring to be heard and your main character's thoughts and views will be crowded out, making it difficult for the reader to follow their progress.

23

Getting to the End

I began this book by advising that you write something every day and, if you've taken that on board, your daily writing habit should by now be firmly entrenched. You will need to draw on that habit when the writing becomes slow, your characters seem ponderous and you're wondering why you ever started. You may feel drained by the whole experience, and if this happens you only need to leave it alone for a few days, keeping the characters in your mind, before things fall back into place. You will return with a refreshed mind and increased energy.

Writer's Block

However, there are times when a break doesn't work. You might feel that you're suffering from writer's block. I have to say straight away that I'm not at all convinced that there is such a thing as writer's block. What I do believe in is a lack of confidence, boredom with the whole process, and a failure to correctly draw characters and their movements within the plot. Over the years I've had many students who began their writing in a feverish air of excitement and at roughly the half-way point in the story, the energy dissipates, their enthusiasm disappears and they tell me they've lost interest in the project.

The problem with calling these difficulties 'writer's block' is that it becomes self-fulfilling: you have this condition therefore you can't write, and you can't write because you have writer's block. What a vicious circle!

Rather than call this 'writer's block', I'd like to focus on what might be the problem. It could be that your plotting has not been done properly, and you may need to do some research to help push your story along. It might be that you do not know where to take your character next. Maybe you've not delved deeply enough into your character's psyche. Go back to your original character sketches.

- Are they superficial?
- Are you getting to the heart of your character?
- Is the problem plotting?

Some people are weaker on characterisation, others not so good with plotting. When plotter's plots go wrong, it's often because they haven't focused on the characters. Conversely, writers who have plenty of character material may find their plots need more development. An easy remedy in either of these two scenarios is to write a bit more, and keep writing until you understand the characters you've created. Plots can be fattened up by more structure, and by this I do not mean shovelling in an immense amount of extra backstory. I admit that my plots are often weak and my way of correcting this is to add complexity, rather than add extra events. By adding complexity, I mean that I often re-visit my early notes, the jottings that I made when I first began to write my story, and check to see what my original thoughts were. It's no secret that very often writers will embark on a new story with a fixed idea of how the story will pan out only to find at the end of the story that it bears little resemblance to the original idea. If that's the case, then I check to see if there is room for greater conflict in my story, maybe the character's reaction to something that has been said can be improved upon. How complex is the relationship between my characters? Can it be made more complex, will that improve the narrative? Do I need to delve deeper, can it be made more challenging?

Don't prop up an ailing plot or character by loading the narrative with extra words in the hope that your reader won't notice – they will. Go back to the beginning, see what needs to be done and do it. You might have reached this far in the book and wonder how many times you will need to re-write. The answer to that is as many times as it takes. Writing is extremely demanding, whether short stories or novels, and if you want to see your work published, you need to get it as good as it can be and that will involve a lot of re-writing.

Sometimes, whatever you try you can't resurrect the original enthusiasm that you had when you embarked on the story. If this is the case I'd strongly recommend walking away from it for a while, not with the intention of giving it up, but with the view of getting some breathing space between you and your story. It might be that you're tired and need to recharge your batteries. Go out for a walk, mow the lawn, walk the dog, but as you do these tasks, keep your story in mind and mull over the problem at hand. You may find that putting some distance between you and your writing is exactly what was needed, and you can return to your story in a more positive frame of mind.

Stamina

To write a story, any story of any word count, requires stamina. Earlier, I stated that students often mistakenly believe that writing short stories is far easier than writing a novel. But just as much stamina is needed for a short story as it is for a novel.

Stamina is required when you grind to a halt, when you can't think of where to go next, and when you're unable to reach a suitable ending. You might find yourself the victim of procrastination. You sit and stare out of the window. You check your emails obsessively, or find tasks that are suddenly essential to your wellbeing.

It might be of some comfort to know that most writers go through this period. Published writers look upon it as rite of passage, something to be got through, tedious as it is.

For the novice writer, I've made a list of some strategies that may help kick start your writing process again.

- **Leave a sentence unfinished**

As humans we are innate problem solvers. When we come back to our writing the next day and find an unfinished sentence, we are overcome with the urge to at least solve the problem of that one incomplete sentence. But by the time we've solved that problem we're caught up in the drama that's on the page and we're spurred on to keep writing.

- **Re-read an earlier paragraph**

By this I mean reading work you've already done, not editing it, merely reading through. By doing this, you can get a sense for what your next step needs to be, and it should inspire you to push on with your work.

- **Time yourself**

Allocate yourself a set amount of time in which to write. Put your watch on the desk and write for an hour. If at the end of the hour you have more to write, give yourself another hour and carry on in this way.

- **Don't edit – yet**

The urge to edit your writing as you go is very hard to overcome, but you must. There's a saying, 'Don't get it right, get it written', and this is a helpful maxim to learn. If you do begin editing half-way through your story, it will seriously hamper you from finishing it. Instead, if you find changes you wish to make, jot down some rough notes and carry on. Keep writing, keep the words flowing. Editing comes later.

'What if'

If you're still stuck after trying all the techniques suggested in this section, you might try the what if technique. I use this often during my classes and it can bring a lot of new ideas and fresh thoughts.

The technique is simple – just ask yourself:

- What if my character broke his leg?
- What if he had an affair?
- What if he lost his job?
- What if he became a father?

Ask questions of your character and see if something occurs to you, some new experience that you can develop, which will bring something deeper to your story.

Isolation

Writing can be incredibly lonely. It's a solitary process. You sit alone at your desk or your kitchen table, or wherever you write, with only your characters for company. You may be lucky and know another writer with whom you can share thoughts and encouragement. You can ask one another, "How many words have you managed today?" A writing friend or writing buddy can be really useful for maintaining motivation – and so can a writers' group.

Writers' groups are found in most towns and cities, where other like-minded people go share their concerns, as well as compare strategies and progress in their writing. If you don't know where to find writers' groups, try your local library because they may have a list of groups. Local adult education centres will have their courses published in their prospectuses, and universities often run creative writing courses. You may have to visit a few groups and classes before you find one that suits you, one where you will be happy to hear others' views on your writing. I firmly believe that in a strong, supportive group, students can learn as much from each other as they can from the tutor.

There are a number of distance learning courses or online writing groups. I have no experience of these but my personal view is that by virtue of the fact that your work is submitted to an unseen tutor, you're not really reducing your physical isolation as a writer.

There are many residential writing courses which take place over a weekend, a week or maybe three or four days. These are often run by published writers who share their own experiences of writing and being published. You may find this stimulating and encouraging, and your enjoyment and enthusiasm will carry through when you return home.

Many writing magazines run adverts for courses and classes. Research them and find something that suits you and your budget. The Arvon Foundation is well known and has had many satisfied writers on its courses. You can find them on www.arvon.co.uk, where they list their centres and prices.

24

Presentation

Presentation is the way you prepare your manuscript for publication, or for a competition, or simply for someone other than yourself to read. Your aim is to make the work as easy to read as possible, and to make the type on the page almost invisible so that the reader can enjoy the content.

When preparing your work, you should aim to get the story looking as good as possible. It might be that you will not be showing your work to anyone other than your family and, even if this is the case, your story still should look first rate. You've worked hard and, when you hold your finished story, you should feel a sense of pride and achievement.

Good layout makes a big difference. A story that is crammed tightly on the page without a lot of white space and few paragraph breaks can look dense and uninviting.

These are my top tips for great manuscript presentation:
* Select a standard serif font
  (they're easier to read than sans serif).
* Use a 12 point type, double line spaced.
* Allow some 'air' around the text by formatting margins

of approximately 2cm left and right.

- Indent the first line of each new paragraph by about 1.5cm.
- Each time a character speaks, indent and give them a fresh line.
- When the person they're talking to speaks, indent again and give them a fresh line. That way there cannot be any confusion about who is speaking.
- To denote that time has elapsed use an extra line space and remove the indent from the first line of the next paragraph.
- Number your pages consecutively, either bottom right or bottom centre.
- Type or print out only on one side of the paper.

Part Three: Markets

25

Writing for Radio

The best advice for anyone learning to write short stories is to read them; likewise, if your dream is to write short stories for radio, then you must listen to them. Listen to the way the story is told and how the characterisation is drawn. Actively seek to understand what makes a story work on radio.

I have had some of my work broadcast in which I wrote in the first person (they're monologues and a lot of radio short stories are done this way). Alan Bennett's hugely successful monologues *Talking Heads* were originally written for television in 1987, but were also broadcast on radio. A monologue allows the listener to get very close to the protagonist, hearing their fears and concerns, and following their progress throughout the length of the story.

Here is an extract from my story *Before I Loved You*:

> *I imagined you at home at night, living in a flat, drinking beer from cans and never, ever did I see you with another girl. What do you do on Saturday nights? Where do you go? Can I come with you? Having you inside my head made me brave, bold,*

*asking questions because there was no fear of
rejection. I began to tell you all about my life at
home, my mum, my dad, the fights I had with my
sister. She borrows my clothes and steals my friends.
She couldn't steal you, you were mine and nobody
knew about you. You always understood, you were
my ally, my secret friend.*

This story came from an idea I had about a lonely woman who fantasises about someone she works with. It was a real thrill to hear my words read aloud by an actor. I entered the story in a competition run by an organization in Plymouth and it was broadcast by BBC Radio Devon in 2008.

Short stories on radio have to be shaped, they need rhythm, and perhaps most importantly of all, they need voices. In the chapter on voice I urged you to think about where your characters come from. If you're planning on submitting a story for broadcast, this is important. You need to develop a clear difference between the characters. Work towards getting the listener to 'see' your characters and the action, and from there they can picture the setting and feel the emotion. If you're planning a monologue, you should aim for a strong, guiding voice, someone who sounds like an individual. Try building your story around such a voice.

A story for radio works best if there are no flashbacks. When the story is linear in structure it's easier to follow. When writing a short story for radio, too many characters can often over-complicate things. If a reader of a short story gets confused about who is speaking, it's a simple matter to turn back the pages and check on who's who. You can't do this if you're listening to it on the radio. Two characters interacting facilitate the simplest, most essential form of dialogue. They create a situation where two people with conflicting desires go head to head and drama is created when their needs clash.

It is worth remembering that when you write for radio, you're writing for performance. Actors are skilled and can add a lot of meaning and nuance to words, but the narrative needs to leave room for them to do so. You might want to consider that when you write for radio, it's best to focus more on the character and less on the plot. Build intensity rather than plot lines. Give your character a single, strong objective. Then introduce an antagonist – another character who opposes the protagonist in some way.

A word of caution: new writers often feel that important information must be told in dialogue. However, expositional dialogue – which tells rather than shows – results in ponderous tension. Good dialogue has to sound like real speech and should have shape and focus. Remember that a character's speech should be going somewhere. They have an aim, an agenda, and their dialogue moves towards that aim. It doesn't stand still.

I've put together a list of what might help when writing for radio:

- Your story should start quickly, clearly and dramatically – it needs to capture the audience in the first 30 seconds (about 100 words). Slow, elegiac writing might not work on radio.
- Characters who speak in different tones are especially effective on radio. Try giving characters different vocabularies, paces and styles of speaking (slow, teasing, childish, bullying, pedantic, and poetic are a few of many examples).
- Avoid dialogue in which questions are asked and answered, or when one character seems to be interviewing another, because this can be very boring to listen to. Each character ought to have their own agenda; no-one is a foil or sounding board for another.
- Remember that people ignore each other in real life. They change the subject, answer questions that are not asked, interrupt each other or themselves, talk over each other, repeat

themselves, speak in incomplete sentences, have pet words or phrases, and they don't always use proper English.

* Use silences. The heavy silence, the pause after a loaded question. 'Where were you last night?'

* Make your characters active. What a character is doing, their physical activity, often works its way into their dialogue. For instance, you might be writing about two characters who are side by side on treadmills, their conversation would be punctuated by breathlessness.

* When you have a piece of information that has to be revealed in dialogue, have characters argue over that piece of information. Find a strong and simple motivation for a character. Maybe someone searching for the book his late father published, now out of print.

* Create a second character who could help the first character fulfil a need.

* Avoid vast timescales and elusive or ambiguous endings. Avoid all repetition – it shows up much more on radio than on paper. The same goes for clichés, which should be avoided or deleted during the editing process.

* Cut, cut and cut again. Write in drafts and then edit them extensively. Remember that what is not said is often more important, and indeed more interesting, than what is said.

* Remember that if your story is successful, it probably will be read by one voice. Short stories as opposed to plays are usually read by one actor who reads all the characters.

I often recommend my students read their work out loud and this is crucial when writing for radio. Even better, record yourself reading your story, listen to the way it sounds. You should listen out for flat sections of narrative, for a voice that doesn't ring true. You need to consider everything you want to do in the light of how it will sound. Shape is an integral part of any short story, and remember that rhythm, shape and voice are especially important in a short story written for radio. Here I mean the beginning, middle and an end, the natural shape of a story. Give some thought to the actor who will be reading your story; try to imagine someone who you think would suit your narrative. Work to that voice, build your words around them.

Another important reason to read your work aloud is to time yourself. You need to know if your story can comfortably fill a 15 minute slot, preferably 12 minutes – is it too long or too short?

Think about your proposed audience, remember that they might well be from a range of ages and backgrounds. You need to be aware that your target audience may be accompanied by small children (at home or on school runs), so avoid using strong language or adult content.

Ask yourself two questions:
- What are people going to think after my story ends?
- What are they going to take away with them?

The BBC has a website for writers: www.bbc.co.uk/writersroom. You will find details about how to submit your work and what stories the BBC is looking for. They will often post themes for stories for submissions, so check the website regularly. It can save time and effort if you check to see if they accept un-solicited queries and manuscripts. I would also advise that you do a little research into who should address your manuscript to, because 'Dear Sir/Madam' may mean your manuscript languishes on a desk unclaimed for weeks before someone has time to pick it up and assess it.

The BBC isn't the only outlet for short stories. Other networks have a short story slot so try them too. If the first story fails to find a home, re-work it and try submitting a short story for publication somewhere else, or have another attempt at writing for radio. Waiting times are long and you must be patient. Stories that have been published can be used on radio. When sending your work in, always enclose a large stamped addressed envelope with enough return postage. That way if your story isn't successful it will come back to you.

26

Writing for Magazines

I would strongly recommend that you buy either the *Writers & Artists Yearbook* or the *Writer's Handbook*. They are published every year and are important sources of information for writers. In these books, you will find details of the magazines that take short story submissions and, importantly, their guidelines. Also listed in these books are details of short story competitions.

If you think your story might be of interest to a women's magazine, such as *Woman's Weekly*, *People's Friend*, or *Best*, my first piece of advice would be to read the magazine and familiarise yourself with the stories that are being published. Don't only read the stories, but look at the general content of the magazine. What kind of features does it run? What kind of age range do you think they'll appeal to? Is it for grandparents, or young couples, maybe home-owners? By doing this you'll get a strong feel for the targeted market of that magazine.

If you think your story is suitable for a more general magazine, the advice is the same: read the magazine first before approaching it with a short story submission. It is best to find out the fiction editor's name and address your letter directly to them. Any time you approach a magazine, always send your story in with a stamped addressed envelope. Most magazines have a webpage and on that page you will usually find their guidelines for writing the stories they will consider.

In addition to giving her advice about word count and the times of the year editors are looking for submissions, Gaynor Davies-Fiction, editor of *Woman's Weekly*, has this to say of the short stories she's looking for:

> *When we choose our stories, we first and foremost try to picture our audience. From our latest research, we know that our readers increasingly cover all ages and all walks of life. What they look for from us is entertainment that isn't going to fill them with shock and horror. But neither are they looking for stories that will send them to sleep!*

When you read the guidelines from various magazines, there will be details on the length of story they will be looking for

Fiction editors are busy people and they don't have the time to spend cutting your over-long story, no matter how good it is. So do yourself a favour and keep to the required word count.

and a long list of what they don't want. On that list will be expletive-soaked language, inclusion of explicit sexual scenes and gratuitous violence. At this point, it is worth stating that you really do need to know your market and work your story around the guidelines provided. Write for the market and, if you find this difficult, then perhaps you should target another magazine or another area medium.

Getting a short story into a magazine isn't easy but you can maximise your chances by doing your research. Check out the magazine where you think your stories will fit in nicely and, once again, if their guidelines ask for stories up to 1,000 words, they will only look at stories with that number. Fiction editors are busy people and they don't have the time to spend cutting your over-long story, no matter how good it is. So do yourself a favour and keep to the required word count.

Although a lot of magazines that publish fiction are aimed at women, men also write short stories for the same market. *Candis* is a new magazine to me but they also publish short stories. Debbie Attewell, fiction editor at *Candis* says, 'I personally read every short story submitted to *Candis*. Each month three from the shortlist are sent out to that issue's reader panelists for their comments and I'll have the deciding vote if necessary. This ensures that the best story with the widest appeal is selected each month.'

Candis target audience is women aged 30–58 as well as their husbands and partners. Their guidelines say they are looking for 'clever, keep-em-guessing story lines, twist in the tale/tales-of-the-unexpected style writing. Short, tightly written whodunits; warm, likeable central characters.'

At the time of writing, the fee is £500 payable on written acceptance which is healthy, but payment for stories in magazines is generally not generous.

■ EXERCISE

In first person write a paragraph about a woman who is preparing to leave her husband. Write about the reasons she is leaving and how she will feel. Read your work aloud and listen to the phrases you've used. If possible, record your work and see how it sounds. Is it engaging? Would you tune in to hear it?

27

Short Story Competitions

If you type 'short story competitions' into your search engine then you will find over a million, and those are only the ones in the UK!

I'm a huge fan of short story competitions as they can help new writers in three ways:
- To write within a specified word count.
- To write to a deadline.
- If your story is selected for a prize, it will boost your self-confidence immeasurably.

Writing is a lonely occupation. With no one to stand over your shoulder and hold you accountable that you finish by a given deadline, there is great danger that the days, weeks, and months will pass without writing anything of note. However, if the rules of the competition say that the entry has to be by the end of June, that will sharpen your resolve, you will work to that deadline. Competition organisers tell me that when the competition is announced, there will be a flurry of entries which they assume are stories that have been languishing in a bottom drawer somewhere, and then, closer to the deadline, there is always an avalanche of stories from writers who have been working to that deadline.

We've discussed writing to a word limit – and there will always be a word limit in short story competitions – and to keep to that limit can be challenging. But as mentioned before, you must adhere to the rules. It is a discipline that can be daunting but is certainly achievable.

Most competitions ask for an entrance fee; these can vary, but they are usually in the £5–£7 region, but I do know of one which asks for £20 as an entry fee. Needless to say the prize money for that competition is generous.

> **Short story competitions can be an excellent way to boost your writing CV, not to mention the monetary prizes and the glory. Just getting onto a longlist or a shortlist is great exposure, even if you don't win.**
> *Tania Hershman*

For most short story competitions, my understanding is that the stories will be read by a team of people who will sort them into various sections. Those that are immediately discounted, those that are possible and those that deserve another reading. Following the initial reading, the hopeful stories will be passed to the competition judge. I've judged short story competitions and I've been amazed at the talent and quality of the entries.

Submissions that don't adhere to the rules of the competition will be immediately rejected. Most competitions ask you to complete an entry form, giving your name, address, email address, telephone number, word count and title of the story.

They insist that nothing other than the page number and maybe the title appear on each page. Certainly do not put your name on it as stories are always judged anonymously.

I hope you enter competitions and I do hope you are

successful. To be awarded a prize, to be long-listed or Highly Commended, maybe even to win outright is a tremendous boost to your morale. But more than that, it's something to add to your writing CV. Being able to tell an agent or publisher that your work has won prizes is important in your quest to be taken seriously as a writer.

Whilst conducting research for this book, I read an article by Tracy Chevalier, who wrote *Girl with a Pearl Earring* and *Remarkable Creatures*. She was the judge for the *Mslexia* short story competition.

When she announced the winner, she also wrote the following:

> *I must confess I was a little disheartened by the quality of much of the writing. Lots of stories had good ideas that were let down by pedestrian prose – too many clichés, too little poetry, too much that was just ordinary.*
>
> *Grammar, punctuation and spelling were often sloppy – and that goes for some of the winners too. Does no one understand how to use commas effectively anymore? Many also found it hard to write a decent ending and simply stopped as if they'd run out of petrol, abandoning the story on the side of the road.*
>
> *I also longed at times to read something extraordinary that would give me a jolt: a character who surprised me, an unusual turn of phrase, a new way of considering one of the old themes of death, loss or love. I wanted to read stories that took risks and felt fresh and different, I felt as if I'd read some version of them before.*
>
> *Am I being a little harsh? Maybe. But so many people write these days, that the competition*

is fierce and if you want to float to the top you have to push yourself in unusual ways to stand out from the crowd.

You will remember that in the chapter on description, I urged you to seek out new descriptions, new angles, and a different slant on your story. Judges, editors, publishers are all searching for originality. Don't fall into a tried and tested trap – make your story different. As Tracy Chevalier says, make it stand out from the crowd.

You must remember that the judging of your stories is subjective: one judge may well think that your story is brilliant and the characterisation is well executed, and another might think that the characters are cardboard and the dialogue forced. What can you learn from this?

First and foremost you have to learn from this. What suits one person may not suit another. It is not unknown for short story entrants to check out who the judges are and, if the judge is a well-known figure, write a story with that person in mind. This cannot be done each time obviously, and it is no guarantee, but it does happen and simply reinforces the fact that what suits one person, may not suit another. If your story fails to gain any recognition in a short story competition, don't discard it. Read it through again. See if it can be improved upon and then send it out to another short story competition. You've got nothing to lose, other than the cost of the entry.

Amongst the rules in most short story competitions, there is a warning: the competition organisers insist that your entry should not be entered for another short story competition simultaneously. Don't think you can get away with it. What would you do if your story gained prizes in both competitions and your lie was found out? Stick to the rules, play the game.

In my own local area there is the Bristol Short Story Prize (bristolprize.co.uk) which is an annual event.

The prizes are extremely generous:

1st prize: £500 plus £150 Waterstones gift card
2nd prize: £350 plus £100 Waterstones gift card
3rd prize: £200 plus £100 Waterstones gift card

The entrance fee for this competition is £7, the word count is 3,000 words and there is no theme. All 20 short listed stories are published in a beautifully-produced paperback anthology.

The Fish short story competition prize has been running for a long time. Details can be found on www.fish.publishing.com. Sean Lusk, a judge of the Fish prize says that the judges are always looking for 'good, literary writing, with a weather eye out for anything that breaks the mould'.

If you subscribe to writing magazines, they too will give details of short story competitions.

Alison Clink, organiser of the Frome Festival Short Story Competition outlines what she likes and doesn't like to see in short story entries:

> *When making up the short lists for the Frome Festival Short Story Competition, the first thing I look for is good writing and a good command of grammar and punctuation. The winning stories will go up on the website with no editing and therefore have to be perfectly written.*
>
> *The subject matter and the theme of the winning stories could be anything – it's the unique stamp that a talented writer puts on their work that makes it a winner.*
>
> *However, good writing alone won't make a winner. The story must also have substance and*

a strong ending. If a brilliant story doesn't end well, it won't make it.

My pet hates are: 1) Stories that read like a synopsis, i.e. they tell rather than show the story. 2) Stories that have to switch points of view in order to show what's happening. 3) Stories where I'm still not sure what the story is about by the second page. Also, I prefer stories that have some kind of relevance. Maybe that's why science fiction and re-telling of fables don't do it for me. But one rule I always stand by is that if a story makes me laugh or cry then it automatically goes through. This doesn't happen very often by the way.

You will see that most of the points raised by Alison have been covered in previous chapters and believe me when I say that I wrote those chapters before I contacted her to ask what she looks for in a short story entry.

At the end of this book there is a list of various competitions together with a list of literary festivals with a note on which ones run short story competitions.

■ EXERCISE

Enter a competition. What do you have to lose? See how you cope with the word count, the deadline.

28

Working Towards Publication

Submitting to Publishers

My stories have appeared in a number of anthologies by publishers including *Libbon*, *The New Welsh Review*, *Route*, *Mslexia* and *Honno*. There is a market out there for short stories and it's worth while investing time to seek out the publishers of anthologies, see what their submission guidelines are and whether you can pitch your story to them. Again, look in the pages of the *Writers & Artists Yearbook* where there will be a list of publishers for you to try.

It's notoriously difficult to get a mainstream publishing deal for your first short stories as an unknown writer, but it's not impossible. Check out the newspapers, invest in subscriptions of writing magazines such as *Writer's News*, keep your eye out the whole time for requests by publishers for submissions of short stories. If you have found a published collection of short stories that you feel are similar to yours, write to the publisher, tell them that you're impressed by the collection and would they be interested in your stories. What have you got to lose?

I've said this before as I feel it is an important point – bear in mind that response to writing is subjective. Nothing appeals to everyone. If one publisher is lukewarm to your submission, then send it to someone else. If one person didn't like it, the chances are that someone else will.

Preparing for Publication

Having spoken already about submitting your stories to various magazines and publishers, my job would not be complete if I did not address the correct way to prepare your story for publication. I've covered the ways to print your story, the need for clear type, numbered pages and proper layout, now I'd like to concentrate on sending your work to a publisher or magazine.

Search through the *Writer's Handbook* for names of the people you're targeting; if at all possible get the name of someone at the company so you can address your covering letter properly. 'Dear Mr Smith,' as opposed to 'Dear Sir/ Madam.' If this information is not in the book, you can look on the publisher's website. An even surer way is to call them and ask for the name of the person who receives manuscript submissions.

You will also need a covering letter. This should be businesslike and professional, beautifully typed and with your address and contact details clearly visible. If you have won a prize for your writing, include that. If you've targeted that particular publisher because you like the anthologies they have published, say so. Under no circumstances write your letter in green ink, put smiley faces on the page or add witty one-liners. I do know of one student who wrote, 'You've read the rest, now read the best'. Needless to say his story was rejected.

Steer clear of telling the publisher that your family loved your story. That carries no weight at all, other than to prove that your family is well meaning. Always enclose a stamped addressed envelope, large enough to hold your story for when it is returned to you; if you don't, the chances are that your story won't be returned.

Don't inform the publisher that you'll be ringing him at the end of the week to discuss your submission – your story is of the utmost importance to you, but low down on the list of the publisher's priorities.

Finally, allow time. Don't make contact until two or three weeks have passed. When you do telephone, remain polite and simply ask if the story has been received.

To clarify:
Do keep your letter to one page
Be succinct but informative
Include your contact details
And enclose a large SASE

Don't make jokes
Make wild claims about your work
Say your family love the story

Be prepared for your work to come back. Before your confidence takes a bashing, bear in mind that virtually every writer has had to deal with rejection. When your work comes back, type out a fresh letter and send your submission to another publisher. It's a good morale-boosting tactic to always have work 'out there'. It can make the rejection feel less painful.

Sometimes a publisher might send back your work with a note explaining that, whilst your story was not suitable for his current criteria, they would like to see your work in future. Always give yourself a pat on the back if this happens. Publishers are busy people and they receive multiple submissions each week, so they rarely bother to say something unless they mean it!

Don't dwell on the rejections, it doesn't necessarily mean that your story isn't good, it simply means that one publisher didn't think it was suitable.

Self-publishing

With developments in 'print on demand' technology, self-publishing is becoming an increasingly popular option for many writers. This is particularly so if your stories are personal or fit a niche interest that a mainstream publisher wouldn't be interested in taking on. In my classes I've had a number of students who wanted to write their stories simply as a record of what had gone on in their lives or their families'. On more than one occasion, students simply wanted to make a record of made-up stories that had intrigued and entertained their children and grandchildren. For these writers, it was enough to write their stories and publish a handful of copies for their families.

Self-publishing means, quite literally, that you publish yourself. Many writers find this extremely liberating, because they can make all the decisions about what goes into the collection of stories, what features on the jacket, and how it's marketed. However, that can be a lot of work for one person to take on. A self-publisher needs to become an expert in typesetting, proofreading, book jacket design, project management, publishing administration, printing, marketing and promotions.

Some writers juggle these roles successfully and have great fun doing so.

Others don't want to be publishers – they are happy to let someone else take on that role. For these writers, they'd prefer to engage other experts to handle the publishing side for them. These experts are called 'publishing services providers' or 'self-publishing companies' and they'll be happy to steer you through the publishing process. My own publisher, SilverWood Originals, offers such publishing services via their SilverWood Books line (www.silverwoodbooks.co.uk) and writers can be confident that a book produced by SilverWood would match the output of mainstream publishing houses – and that's really important in a world where 'self-publishing' sometimes equals 'amateur'.

These days, self-publishing is beginning to lose this reputation, but slowly, and if a writer wishes to confidently market their books in the retail sector, then they need to produce a high quality product for which readers will be happy to hand over £8.99 or more.

On that point, it is worth remembering that, when choosing to self-publish or buy into professional services, you should not make your decision on the basis of costs alone. You're entering a crowded and competitive market place and if you want booksellers to stock your book, it must be professionally edited, typeset and designed and then printed to the highest quality you can afford. Your book must look like a mainstream publisher produced it. If your intention is to sell your collection of stories, then it really is in your best interest to achieve the polished appearance of a collection of stories that appears on the shelves of your average High Street booksellers.

Finally, you should feel the same sense of pride whether your anthology is self-published or published by a mainstream publisher. It represents a lot of hard work and you'll want that hard work to be reflected in the quality of the finished product.

Final Word

I do hope that this book has been of some help to you. I've been a fan of short stories for a long time, I enjoy the challenge, the confines of the word count, the editing, the struggle to make each word count, to satisfy either a competition judge or a publisher. I read as many short stories as I can, gaining knowledge and understanding with each one, as well as a hefty dose of envy at the writer's skill.

Short stories are difficult to write; they demand a lot from a writer but I believe they are more than worth the effort involved. I can't teach you how to write, but hopefully I've helped to make the process of writing short stories a little less daunting.

I've said that writing short stories is far harder than writing novels; the struggle to polish every word, to make it work for its inclusion in a story, is a real labour of love, but one I hope you will find worthwhile. The knowledge that other people have read my work and hopefully enjoyed what I've written is a feeling I very much enjoy.

Carolyn Lewis
Bristol 2012

Appendix 1: short story competitions

BBC National Short Story Award
Word count: 8,000
Website: www.theshortstory.org.uk/nssp/

Biscuit Publishing International Short Story Prize
Word count: 1,000–5,000
Address: Biscuit Publishing, PO Box 123, Washington,
Tyne & Wear NE37 2YW
Website: www.biscuitpublishing.com

Bridge House Short Story Competition
Word Count: 5,000
Website: www.bridgehousepublishing.co.uk/competition.aspx

Bridport prize
Word count: 5,000
Address: The Bridport Prize, PO Box 6910, Dorset DT6 9BQ
Website: www.bridportprize.org.uk

The Bristol Short Story Prize
Word count: 3,000
Address: Bristol Short Story Prize, Unit 5–16, Paintworks, Bath
Road, BRISTOL, BS4 3EH
Website: www.bristolprize.co.uk

Calderdale short story competition
Word count: 3,000
Address: Short story competition, Central Library, Libraries, Museums and Arts, Northgate, Halifax HX1 1UN
Website: www.calderdale.gov.uk/community/libraries/readers/short story

Chapter One Promotions
Word count: 2,500
Website: www.chapteronepromotions.com

Cooldog Publications
Word count: 3,000
Address: Cooldog Publications, PO Box 2851, Bristol. BS6 9GJ
Website: www.cooldog.co.uk/

Dark Tales Short Story Competition
Word count: 5,000
Address: Dark Tales Short Story Competition, 7 Offley Street, Worcester, WR3 8BH
Website: www.darktales.co.uk/contest.php

Exeter Writers Short Story Competition
Word count: 3,000
Address: Exeter Writers, 202 Manstone Avenue, Sidmouth, Devon, EX10 9TL
Website: www.exeterwriters.org.uk

Fish Publishing Short Story Competition
Word count: 5,000
Address: Fish Publishing, Durrus, Bantry, Co. Cork, Ireland
Website: www.fishpublishing.com

Frome Festival Short Story Competition
Word count: 1,000–2,200 words
Address: Frome Festival short story competition c/o Frome library, Justice Lane, Frome, Somerset BA11 1BE
Website: www.fromefestival.co.uk

Giggle Magazines' Short Story Competition
Word Count: 1,000
Address: The Coal Exchange, Mount Stuart Square, Cardiff Bay, CF10 5EB
Website: www.giggle-magazine.co.uk

Hay on Wye Short Story Prize
Word count: 2,000
Theme: Avarice
Address: Hay & District Community Support, Oxford Road, Hay-on-Wye, HEREFORD, HR3 5AL
Website: www.hayonwyeshortstory.com

Highlands & Islands Short Story Association
Word count: 2,500
Address: 20 Lochslin, Balintore, Easter Ross, Scotland IV20 1UP
Website: www.hissac.co.uk

Legend Writing Awards
Word count: 2,000
Address: Legend Writing Award, 39 Emmanuel Road, Hastings, East Sussex, TN34 3LB
Website: www.legendwritingaward.com

The New Writer Short Story Competition
Word count: 4,000
Address: The New Writer, PO Box 60, Cranbrook,
Kent, TN17 2ZR
Website: www.thenewwriter.com

Spilling Ink Review Short Story Competition
Word Count: 3,000
Address: Spilling Ink, PO Box 16864, Glasgow, G11 9DJ
Website: www.spillinginkreview.com/competitions

V S Pritchett Memorial Prize
Word count: between 2,000 and 5,000 words
Address: The Royal Society of Literature, Somerset House,
Strand, London WC2R 1LA
Website: www.rslit.org

Wells Festival of Literature Short Story Competition
Word count: 1,800–2,000
Address: Short Story Competition, Chegworth House, Moor
Lane, Draycott, Cheddar, Somerset BS27 3TD
Website: www.wlitf.co.uk/story rules

The Writers Bureau Short Story Prize
Word count: 2,000 words
Address: Sevendale House, 7 Dale Street, MANCHESTER, M1
1JB
Website: www.wbcompetition.com

Yeovil Literary Prize
Word count: 2,000
Address: Yeovil Prizes 2010, The Octagon Theatre, Hendford,
Yeovil BA20 1DC
Website: www.writing.competition.co.uk

Appendix 2: literary festivals

Althorp Literary Festival
This festival is usually held on the second weekend in June each year.
Website: www.althorp.com/literary.php
 Or you can email: events@althorp.com

Appledore Book Festival
[This festival includes readings and lectures by writers from every kind of genre; from children's authors to biographers to screen writers to novelists and storytellers.]
Website: www.appledorebookfestival.co.uk

Bath Literature Festival
10 days of literary events: A number of workshops are available on subjects like how to write a book and how to edit books for publication.
Website: www.bathfestivalsorg.uk

Bridport Literary Festival
Festival normally runs between October and November. A short story competition is part of the festivities.
Website: www.bridport.arts.com

Edinburgh International Book Festival
This has become the largest festival of its kind in the world. Each year there are 'meet the author' events. Normally held in August.
Website: edbookfest.co.uk

Frome Festival
A festival in July every year that also includes a short story competition.
Website: www.fromefestival.co.uk

The Guardian Hay Festival
Non-profit festival that has expanded around the world in recent years. Appearances by celebrity guests, musical performances and some of the world's most renowned authors.
Website: www.hayfestival.co.uk

Humber Mouth Literature Festival
Wide ranging event with speakers like Kate Long and Kate Atkinson.
Website: www.humbermouth.org.uk

Manchester Literature Festival
In 2008, the festival included 120 writers from all over the world. There is opportunity to meet favourite authors.
Website: www.manchesterliteraturefestival.co.uk

The Reading Festival of Crime
Author talks, panel discussions and competitions from the best international, national and local crime authors.
Website: www.readingfestivalofcrimewriting.org.uk/

The Swindown Festival of Literature
New writers, terrific speakers, and a fantastic celebration for Swindon of things well written and things well said.
Website: www.swindonfestivalofliterature.co.uk/

The Times Cheltenham Literature Festival

The festival had over 450 authors in 2008, participating in more than 350 events.

Details from: Christin Stein – Festival organiser

Email: christin.stein@cheltenhamfestivals.com

Wells Festival of Literature

Lectures by authors and poets. The festival also runs a short story competition.

Website: www.wlitf.co.uk

Winchester Writers' Conference Festival and Book Fair

The line up includes novelists, poets, producers, literary agents and commissioning editors.

Website: www.writersconference.co.uk

As any sensible writer will know, you are advised to carefully check for yourself the details of all short story competitions before entering, and investigate literary festivals before making a decision about which, if any, to attend.

Lightning Source UK Ltd.
Milton Keynes UK
UKOW030639180612

194583UK00001B/2/P